White Magic

Money and to Defeat the Negative Energy

(The Complete Book of White Magic for Novices in Wicca)

Harvey Whyte

Published By **Elena Holly**

Harvey Whyte

All Rights Reserved

White Magic: Money and to Defeat the Negative Energy (The Complete Book of White Magic for Novices in Wicca)

ISBN 978-1-77485-729-8

No part of this guidebook shall be reproduced in any form without permission in writing from the publisher except in the case of brief quotations embodied in critical articles or reviews.

Legal & Disclaimer

The information contained in this ebook is not designed to replace or take the place of any form of medicine or professional medical advice. The information in this ebook has been provided for educational & entertainment purposes only.

The information contained in this book has been compiled from sources deemed reliable, and it is accurate to the best of the Author's knowledge; however, the Author cannot guarantee its accuracy and validity and cannot be held liable for any errors or omissions. Changes are periodically made to this book. You must consult your doctor or get professional medical advice before using any of the suggested remedies, techniques, or information in this book.

Upon using the information contained in this book, you agree to hold harmless the Author from and against any damages, costs, and expenses, including any legal fees potentially resulting from the application of any of the information provided by this guide. This disclaimer applies to any damages or injury caused by the use and application, whether directly or indirectly, of any advice or information presented, whether for breach of contract, tort, negligence, personal injury, criminal intent, or under any other cause of action.

You agree to accept all risks of using the information presented inside this book. You need to consult a professional medical practitioner in order to ensure you are both able and healthy enough to participate in this program.

TABLE OF CONTENTS

Introduction 1

Chapter 1: The Witches"Talents 4

Chapter 2: The Importance Of Study 26

Chapter 3: Spell Crafting 42

Chapter 4: Rituals 50

Chapter 5: Dark Witchcraft 64

Chapter 6: Daily Practice 81

Chapter 7: Other Words 116

Chapter 8: Internal Works 126

Chapter 9: Preparing For Ritual 144

Chapter 10: Purifying Purification 156

Conclusion 182

Introduction

In the modern world the word "pagan" is used to refer to witchcraft that is dark. The truth is that pagans of old lived according to what is known as the Laws of Nature. Modern Pagans aren't one-dimensional: some use dark magic, while others are practicing white magic. However, ancient wisdom is preserved and improved by modern technology.

At the time I was born, my nation was under communist administration. In the eyes of the communist agenda, God doesn't exist. There is nothing supernatural. We had to live our lives as if we were living double lives. We practiced hiding in the shadows and did our best to keep our mouths shut.

We were fortunate to live in a small city that was surrounded by farms. The prohibitions on religion were relaxed. The people prayed in closed rooms and discussed God inside their kitchens. They also discussed witches. Like in every small town, people solve their problems by going to witches.

My bloodline is derived from an ancient Pagan tribe that believed in Svarog, the Old god of the Sun. It's a proto-Slavic group that was settled during the second millennium B.C. and was transformed to Christianity during about the time of the 12th century. The conversion did not go according to the plan, but. It was not as expected. Eastern Orthodox religion became a combination with Christianity along with Paganism. Older rituals were merged together with Christian rituals.

The witches were always present. Within The Eastern Orthodox religion witch hunts were never a thing, and Slavic witchcraft secrets weren't lost. Slavic witches have been collecting wisdom about magic for thousands of years. "Witch" is the word that "witch" means in Slavic language literally translates to "the one who is knowledgeable," "the wise one." Witches were considered to be feared and were left to perform their craft.

They were also the first to be scientists. They were the first doctors and first physical scientists. The oldest profession isn't "ladies who sleep." It's us as witches, shamans and witches. They are the wise. In tribes unaffected by the modern world there is no prostitution however witches and shamans do.

Chapter 1: The Witches"Talents

The Bible states that all of us have different abilities to serve the Kingdom of God and are all going to have jobs in Heaven. Spirits who return to God after we die will have different abilities and occupations. There are some lucky witches who discover at an early age which their spiritual abilities and professions are. My cousin is one of these. Olga.

Olga

Olga is the person she "sees the people." She reaches deep into one's mind and is able to determine the person's true identity the person is, as well as their hidden fears and their joys.

Olga is known as a social butterfly. Her life isn't extravagant and she's simply over the moon. What can ordinary people do when they step onto an airplane? They attempt to relax and sleep and hope to arrive intact. But not while Olga is present.

It is a miracle that she can be seated next to every person in the airplane and speak to them. After five hours of flight, she has the names of everyone and their life stories. There will be laughter and taking pictures, forming groups, and maybe drinking. They will welcome half her plane's passengers to remaining half, and tell individuals that they must be business partners and that others should be best friends or even get married.

And, years later she says to her me, years later: "Would you believe who I have met today? Did you remember in 1990 when we rode that bus to a resort on the lake? It was that woman. ..."

My eyes are blank: "How do you remember everybody on the bus? It was more than a decade ago. I can only recall the moment when the driver was furious at us for having started an alcohol and dancing party. He threatened to take out of our bus."

Nowadays, Olga is an eminent proprietor of a hair salon in a city. This is at first glance.

However, even though regular clients receive regular haircuts from Olga's staff, a select group of people make appointments for private sessions with Olga due to various reasons.

Witches have learned cut hair cutting is an mystical ritual that should not be done lightly. We'll talk more about cutting hair later. When cutting hair of someone else and conversing, Olga goes into their unconscious and looks around for trouble spotsthat she will always find. The subconscious is like a locked room. it could be clean or it could be messy or messy, but you're not getting into. However, Olga with her magical key will identify the issue whether it's a block in the mind or fear. She will then perform the ritual and then poof! The room is clean.

Olga doesn't advertise her services, and she doesn't accept walks-ins. It's like a private club where one cannot be identified with. She's a hit with businessmen, politicians and people who work in the entertainment business. She is also very expensive thanks.

A sad and funny Story

One day, I called Olga and asked her, "Guess what?"

"You're expecting," she said. "And the wife of your brother's spouse is also expecting. She'll be having a baby boy within two weeks of you."

When I spoke to my mother I congratulated her for becoming a double-grandma very soon. My mother then called my brother to congratulate him on becoming father. The phone was on speaker so that his spouse could listen to. My brother was in a state of confusion. My sister-in-law was furious. She had not spoken to him, or anyone else but she was planning to surprise her family. Both were interested in what my mom could be aware of the pregnancy.

"Olga said to Elena that she had told her, and Elena said," she answered.

My brother told me he'd never speak to Olga or me again. My brother's son, who is two weeks younger than my daughter.

Me

According to Olga my talents and work has been described by Olga as "seeker/explorer." It's me who is the person who asks questions, and then gets the answers. I challenge the boundaries of what's recognized and extend my vision to the boundaries of the. How do I accomplish this? What is the process? Old Gods talk to me. (Just kidding.) The reason is that my subconscious mind is in connection to my Spirit of who I am. And the more I make use of this connection, the more powerful it becomes.

Two key aspects contribute to my talents asking the right questions and receive the answers. The second aspect is more crucial. It's easy to ask questions But hearing the answer is more complicated. You must be present and not let my thoughts run through my mind.

Sometimes, an answer is formed in the form of an idea. For instance, if I'm taking a look at an interview, or listening to podcasts, and the host asks questions I can answer the question before anyone has even said the word. It can be frustrating I love imagining the outcome of the movie or book. However, surprises are not often seen.

My little girl: "I can't find my earrings."

My response: "Look inside a shoe." The earrings are there, and it's surprising nobody.

Sometimes, I receive responses visually or by a tangible object. They are typically delayed. I'll be watching TV and somebody will say something that is a precise answer to my query. Maybe you've seen it in a film? They didn't just make it out of thin air. There are many people who has this ability.

It was a great podcast in which the host was speaking about being content with who you are. According to him that you don't need to work on improving yourself. You should just be happy with yourself and your life exactly as it is.

My room is empty: "But what if I love to learn and exercise? Does this mean that I don't like my life the way that I do?"

Podcasts: "If you exercise and take on new challenges because you love doing it, then good for you. This doesn't mean that you aren't enjoying yourself."

It's there. I'm good. Thanks, Universe.

When I have a problem and it is a problem, the Universe usually responds to me with a whisper "say that" or "look here." When the wind smashed my fence in the garden and I wondered, "Where should I get new fencing, or what sort of fence would I want?" The next time I looked at the feed on my Instagram feed, I noticed ads for fences I loved. I am in the process of getting the fence I want now.

Answers are found from billboards or books. Sometimes, it's a conversation that was overheard at a store. There are times when it's a telephone call or an email. And they're pouring, each and every minute.

I'm not sure how it feels to live without God's direction. I'd be lost, without being able to know the right way to go. Is the entire world lost?

What can you do with this data? I will add parts to the puzzle I refer to as the Universe. The puzzle is infinite by size and pieces, and is made up of endless layers. Complex, yet exciting. There's a lot to discover! Also my skills are helpful when I teach novice witches. They may have a million questions, yet we always find solutions for their issues.

I make use of my knowledge to improve my life. It only took me several minutes to make the move from a small city in the former communist state to the beach town of California. My old neighbors still draw water from wells. Their bathrooms are in the soil. Each one of them is a unique talent. In the market, I usually look around hoping to spot somebody from back home. Maybe, one day, I will.

Aunt Lyuba

Aunt Lyuba has had a difficult life and continues to suffer for performing dark magic. I'm grateful for her advice. She taught us not to fall into the dark side.

We aren't sure of Aunt Lyuba's talents are because she was on the dark side before we began our training. Olga states that all she sees inside Aunt Luyba's mind is darkness.

Aunt Lyuba is a witch of the night who performs black magic old fashion by using blood, potions as well as spell satchels and shabashes. In Slavic custom, shabash refers to an assembly of forces from the dark such as demons, witches, and other creatures, perhaps maybe Lucifer himself. Don't confuse witches' shabbash with Jewish Shabash.

Aunt Lyuba is my father's younger sister. The father of my dad was eldest of seven children. According to my relatives and aunts Lyuba got married happily and had two gorgeous children when she started to be fascinated by the world of magic. It was later revealed to be dark magic. She soon lost her husband due to divorce. People began to pay for her magical services.

When Alexander, her son Alexander was just sixteen He was detained for assault and sentenced to two years in prison. Then he went into jail and released. Between prison sentences, he had the chance to have one daughter, but lost her after being exiled to another country. She's an adult now but hasn't had a contact with her dad since.

As I type this the aunt Lyuba was in her mid-sixties, however, she looks 90 like a film witch would. She's getting worse and is losing her sight. Yet she continues to practice witchcraft. We believe that the grief that befell aunt Lyuba and her children stemmed from the dark realms.

The majority of witches turn into dark witches without realizing it because of an error. It is because they weren't taught magic, and were forced to work it out for themselves. However, they must remember that the Law of Magic says: "There is no escape away from the evil side."

Dark witch's energy differs from the white witch's energy. Dark witchcraft is more powerful. The power that witches get through dark witchcraft alters their power for the duration of time. It causes sorrow, suffering, and tragedy.

Natasha's Story

The daughter of Lyuba Natasha disappeared at the age of thirteen. We waited a year for no contact with her. Lyuba believed she was alive, but in the midst of a difficult situation. One day, Aunt Lyuba was waiting at my door, happy. She knew exactly where Natasha was I was told by her however, I needed to join her, as it was only me the person who could locate her.

"Together with white and dark magic we will be able to locate her. I followed her whereabouts Now it's time for the white magician," she said. I was just sixteen years old.

She drove me to the bus station in the city. It was a long time we looked around the food court and rest areas, waiting areas and the police station bathrooms, and showers. Aunt Lyuba presented Natasha's photograph to everyone.

In the restroom for women I was noticed by an attendant. "Your group is taking showers," she told me. I wasn't sure what she was referring to. In the entryway to the showers, two ladies were talking. When they saw me, one of them shouted, "Hurry, we're leaving shortly."

I'm not sure what the reason but I did open one of the stalls doors. It was Nastasha. I began shouting, "She's here! It's her!" I ran from the bathroom, and came across Aunt Lyuba chatting to two officers. "She's there!" I screamed. Aunt Lyuba was staring at me with an awful feeling of. Why didn't she seem as happy like I was?

The girls were being taken through our city, but had stopped for a bathroom break. By the dark power of her Aunt Lyuba had spotted they were at the railway station.

Natasha was an entire year as a sex victim in one Arabic places where blonde as well as blue eyed girls were prized assets. After an examination, we were informed that Natasha could never be able to have children because of the abuses committed to her. She was fourteen years old. She has never talked about the time of her life that was for us a year away but for her, it was always there.

Aunt Lyuba has never explained to me the reason that I had been the only one to search for Natasha and I have did not ask.

Victor's Story

According my cousin Olga her mother aunt, my Aunt Valya is a witch who is and is in denial. Aunt Valya is the sister of my father. Victor was Olga's elder brother. He passed away at the age of 40 due to unknown causes. Olga says that their mother is responsible for the death of Victor.

In the years following her divorce and her aunt Valya began dating an individual. They soon became serious and began to meet the families of each other. After their first meeting Olga cautioned everyone to stay clear of this man. It was an issue of life or death, she told the group that it was clear that the person had a energetic vampire.

According to Olga the man ought to be dead by now. The people around him suffered curious deaths that seemed unrelated even though he remained alive. He used people's energy to live, Olga was convinced. Aunt Valya was adamant about calling Olga insane and became in love with the vampire. The romantic relationships between vampires and witches are not unusual. Witches, after all, can harness a lot of energy. Aunt Valya has, however, denied that she was witch.

One day, aunt Valya requested Victor to drop off something at the vampire's house. He was sick and needed assistance. The moment Aunt Valya arrived at the house she discovered their son's body on the floor , and the vampire was still sick in the bed.

Medical tests found no cause for the death of Victor. There was no sign of any injury or struggle. Therefore, even though Victor was perfectly healthy and was in good health, the authorities were forced to believe that the cause was natural. The vampire, however recuperated from his illness. After a decade, Aunt Valya remains at his the side of his.

Uncle Nikolai, The Saint

Uncle Nikolai isn't a witcher He was a man of the land, but he suffered the unfortunate experience of getting married to Aunt Valya. He is Olga's father. I'm unable to tell you whether the deceased or alive. I've been to three his funerals. At the time I last heard, he was doing well.

When Uncle Nikolai was married to Aunt Valya He was a responsible and reputable policeman. After a few years of the marriage however he began to drink. They had two small youngsters, Olga and Victor. Nikolai's drinking deteriorated each year, and eventually the teen was violent. He was dismissed from his job, and never to return.

In the wake of Nikolai's drunken behavior violent storms came through every week. Aunt Valya and the children went to the farm of Grandma Polya. Uncle Nikolai did not venture near the farm. He was terrified about his sister-in-law. He was known to call her "old witch." I couldn't figure out the reason.

Grandma Polya, I would discover is a witch of white who had an ability to cook and nature. She was a sweet petite lady sporting an apron as well as a taut gray bun. She was a soft-spoken, cheerful lady. Her home was always smelling of delicious food. The farm was small, but contained different worlds. The ducks and chickens clucked, and the ducks quacked around the backyard. Large piglets and rabbits were spotted in the fields. Beyond the shady forest was a swathe of fishponds with the smallest wooden rowboat. It was a perfect spot for children witches to practise their craft without eye-rolling eyes.

Uncle Nikolai was later arrested for a minor crime. He died in jail. He was burial at the end of the day of his life according to the tradition. As we entered the prison and were shown a grave that had the name of his brother and a cross. Aunt Valya offered an oath. There was no one else to say anything.

Around a year later, we received a notice from the jail of Uncle Nikolai was scheduled to be released shortly. After some questions, it was found the issue was due to a mistake. A different person was burial in the grave with a cross. Uncle Nikolai was released from prison and moved to live at home with his mom.

A few months later, we received an email from the police saying that Uncle Nikolai's body had been discovered inside the morgue. Then, at the time we got there there was an empty grave marked with the cross and the name of Uncle Nikolai on the grave. Another funeral. A few days after Uncle Nikolai was found in his usual drunken state at the usual drinking establishment with his friends.

Then came a telephone call from the mother of Uncle Nikolai informing us that he had been murdered and was laid to rest. The grave of his remains was located within the nearby cemetery, if we wanted to visit. We did. There was a grave that had an inscription of his name on it. His mother would not be able to make a mistake and we believed. The third time is always a charm.

A couple of months later, around time of daybreak, the doorbell at my front came up. Uncle Nikolai was alive and drunk and drunk, was looking for money for transportation to his mom's house. Food, too. Perhaps a drink. I was not surprised by any of it. He looked happy.

Ich called Olga for her to tell her Christ was raised, and again.

Every year, we got contradictory news reports about Nikolai's death and resurrected. The family was of the opinion that someone had placed a spell over Nikolai. Who was the culprit and what spellwas used, we don't know.

My Mother The Dark Widow

My mother isn't a witch. The atheist she is. My father, however was the witcher. He was the mother's first husband. She would then bury the bodies of five. She doesn't believe in the supernatural.

I know why my father captivated my mother. She's one of the rare women who appear to be basic, but can make men turn their heads. This isn't magic or a fable. It's like men can sense the ideal woman on a fundamental level. They are unable to explain why they love each other.

As a young child, I noticed that my mom stood out from all other mother's. I was playing outside with my friends as I watched my mom leave a bus and stroll towards her home. The men in our vicinity were watching her. People on the bus as well as men in the cars that passed by and men in the street, or sitting in their yards, all were looking at my mother. I was initially thinking that something was not correct But then my witching began to take over and I got the answer that they all saw an ideal woman.

The way she moved and moved her body, her movements were captivating. She was a lazy cat-like grace. In a state of ignorance to the impact she had on men she was in her own private world. There were men who were troublesome but she was only aware of them in a hesitant way.

One time, a lady from the next street came by our front door and asked me to call my mother. I replied that she was not at home. The woman asked me to come in, and she was crying. She explained her husband was divorcing her due to his love for my mother. I remember her face and her eyes filled with tears, and her eyes looking at me like she was going to inquire about the reason.

"Why do you think he loves her? He's not even pretty!"

I was 15. I stood in silence I didn't know how to address the woman so desperate to stay with the man that my mother likely did not realize existed.

My mother was sixty when she turned the age of sixty at the time, she went on an "memory" tripto visit locations from her previous. After she reached the home of my childhood she made me an email.

"A stranger stopped me at the old home," she said. "He addressed the name of my mother and informed me that he remembered me. I'm not sure who is he." It's more than 30 years since we left the home.

I can't recall the funeral of my father. I was just four when he passed away in a car crash. Twenty years later, my aunt Lyuba informed me that more than 12 witches attended the funeral. Some were relatives but some were weren't. Some were furious at my mother for having her father was married to an non-witch. Witches are difficult to come across and a marriage between a witcher and a witcher is like an royal wedding.

Aunt Lyuba does not know who placed an evil curse over my mum. The curse was not lifted because only the witch that created the curse could return it.

The second husband of my mother had been poisoned by the ex-wife of his. Three and four of them died from heart ailments. The fifth one died from cancer. A sixth was in prison for beating his ex-wife. On the day he was arrested, my mother threw him out on the streets.

She's in her late 60s now she is probably with a partner or in between them. In a recent phone conversation she mentioned she'd received a wedding proposal from a neighbor who was 10 years older. She turned it down because she thought that he was too old and sick, and required nurses and maids. She isn't interested in being either.

My mom doesn't believe in the power of magic or God. She believes she's unlucky when it comes to males.

Chapter 2: The Importance Of Study

A new witch, who is beginning her journey, initially doesn't understand what's going on around her. She used to know what was right and wrong. In this magical world there is a change in everything. Lines become blurred and meanings are ambiguous. Labels are dissolved. Signs can be interpreted as portents. The symbols are the latest.

A lot of people don't have the time to learn about the art of magic. They lack time, and don't want to put in the effort. They are looking for results immediately! They get them however, they don't get what they were hoping for. They pay a high cost.

When things go wrong anger and resentment are the result. The sooner or later, the negative feelings are able to work their magic. An ordinary person grieves and drinks, then visits counsellors. However, a witch who already summoned Power to play released an unruly troll into her home.

Magic is not a series of tricks. The simple act of gathering a few crystals or lighting candles, and then searching for words online will result in at best situations the same result, but nothing. If the situation isn't so great be prepared for the unexpected.

How Are You?

You are a spirit in the human body, not the reverse. There is nothing such as a living human body with no Spirit inside it. There are those with "lost souls" disengaged from who they actually are, yet the Spirit is still theresomewhere, in deep.

The hierarchy is as follows:

God and Universe The Universe and God can be interchangeable since God is present in every atom. There is anything in this Universe which God "hasn't had a hand on."

Higher World is a vast area that is high frequency energy. The Higher Beings that inhabit it are more closely connected to God and possess greater power than the lower Beings.

Lower World is a vast field of low-frequency, or negative energy. Habitatted by lower beings.

Power - energy that is always is. Higher Beings utilize higher power (Power of Light) and Lower Beings use lower power (Power of Darkness).

Spirit Spirit "child from God" within our lives, created by God's image. Every human being is created "in the likeness God" God," which makes us distinct from animals. Each human being is a Spirit. We communicate with God through our spirits. Spirit is able to connect with the Higher Power or Lower Power. Consider it as a an upward connection to either the higher or lower Worlds as well as to God. Spirituality isn't affected by external sources like other persons or the events.

Humanity is the human point of entry between metaphysical and physical spiritual realms. Humans reside in"the "Middle Earth."

Soul - horizontal energy link to the Middle World. Soul is greatly affected by external influences like people and events. It reacts to the positive or negative energy in the world around us. Soul is our thoughts and emotions. Through Soul that we can connect with Spirit.

Subconscious mind - the place where all the mind-work happens.

Conscious Mind - a means that the unconscious can communicate. The majority of humans have it broken.

Let's tie it all up.

Conscious Mind Subconscious Mind and Soul, then Spirit. Spirit connects the Lower World or Higher World. If it's Higher World then the connection is to God and the Universe.

Now, in different terms:

I am thinking I have thoughts.

My thoughts travel through my subconscious, where they filter through my thoughts, beliefs and experiences.

My soul is a reaction to my thoughts that are filtered and alters my energy frequency according to (feelings).

My Spirit takes in an energy message and matches it with the appropriate Power frequency. For me, it's Power of Light.

-- Power of Light reacts to my energy and alters it into a (Middle) World around me.

Be aware that many things could happen between "I think about thoughts" and "changed world." The subconscious thoughts and emotions can affect the direction of Spirit and the power.

Each human being has the ability to connect with their own Spirit and, through it, become connected with Power. Certain people are more connected. Some are completely disengaged like the black negative holes. They are with a connection by the Spirit or they attain the connection through their practicing.

What is a Witch?

Witches are connected with her spirit. Note: A witch doesn't have control over energy, she's energy. In order to alter the flow of energy, she is an energy flow.

We could say it in different ways:

A witch can't control Power She is Power.

The witch isn't in control of Nature she's Nature.

Why? because you're a Spirit first , and only human being by God's grace. God. Consider yourself one of them.

Question: I'm an aspiring witch. How can I strengthen my connection with the Power greater?

It is necessary to contemplate to discover Nothingness or the Uncontained. It's a space that is full of potential. It's in between thought and breath. The longer you are there, the more easy it will be to get into Nothingness again. This is where the you can communicate with your Spirit. It is also where you can create.

Question: When in life should a witch begin to train?

From the moment they are born. Children have strong connections to Spirit because their unconscious minds aren't yet fully developed. They don't know what's achievable in this world. They don't realize that they aren't capable of doing something. Believe in the magic of, and they believe that anything is possible.

As we get older our minds are tainted with the endless "impossibilities," so we cease believing and lose faith. The older we begin to exercise more, and the harder it will be to change the mind of our subconscious. It's not impossible, but it's not.

White Witch, Dark Witch

White magic can create. Dark magic eliminates.

The difference lies in the energy source. Witches of the White side are able to draw Power of Light through their Spirits. Dark witches draw the Power of Darkness through their Spirits.

Humans are equipped with a radar that can discern the kind of energy field is surrounding them. The radar that detects this is called emotions and feelings. It's also referred to as Soul. Higher frequencies are associated with positive feelings, while lower frequencies bring negative emotions.

Dark witches are usually more powerful than white witches but there's a lot of them. Why? because The Power of Darkness is abundant and easily available. Do you keep an eye on the news? What's the proportion of positive news against. bad news? This tells you a lot about the energy environment we reside in.

It is much more difficult for witches to establish a direct connection to that Power of Light. She needs to eliminate the negative thoughts and blockages from her mind and raise her Spirit's frequency to the same energy associated with The Power of Light.

To help a dark witch align her Spirit's energy frequency to the Lower World? Switch on the TV, or contemplate a negative thought. Easy.

At first look, white witches are far outnumbered. The majority of witchcraft performed all around us involves dark magic. White witches aren't going to even engage in witchcraft that is dark, not even to get rid of the curse, since it's an entirely different type of energy. A lot of times white witches can't help, as she is using an energy frequency that is different.

However, all is not lost for witches of white. Protection spells keep dark magic away. Spells to boost health, prosperity and abundance are in the territory of white witches.

Most importantly, When a White Witch develops a an intense connection to that Power of Light, she is more effective than the army of witches who are dark. This is because this Power of Light comes from the Higher World that's closer to God in its frequency of energy.

There are only a handful of strong white witches in the world and an abundance of powerful dark witches. Dark witches can cause chaos for human beings, yet they're minuscule when compared to the things white witches are able to do. White witches with power can alter the world at a global level as well as altering the reality. This is one of my favorites.

If you're traveling on the same flight with white witches, take a break and relax and nothing bad could occur. If you are living next to the white witch, good for you. No natural disasters will affect you. You'll experience peace and peace of mind.

God and the Church

This is a very crucial. I often talk about God and cite Scriptures from the Bible within this work. Yes, witches of the white race attend church and are involved in rituals of the church.

White witches are Christian who lives according to the Laws of Nature. White witches do nothing that is contrary to Bible's teachings.

Dark witches face dispute with the Church because their actions cause harm. White witches aren't in a conflict. There are no church rituals that harm white witches. The cross, holy water, and religious rituals are just as beneficial to white witches just in the same way as everybody else. Actually, the use of holy water during magic rituals can be beneficial.

I have seen some dark witches at church. Also, I suspect that modern churches are becoming less and less effective. Sunday services tend to be more of an entertainment rather instead of a religious occasion. The essence of the Divine has gone. I believe that is the case only in old churches that have been around for centuries. Modern mega churches? You can forget about it. These are the most popular locations for energy vampires and money-spypers. I've heard of. I've visited.

Witches consider themselves "spiritual" and only. They do not have faith in God and/or the Devil. That's a form of modern witchcraft I'm not in accordance with. I'm an old-fashioned witch.

There are witches too who are believers in Devil and the darkness, but not God. The witches I have encountered puzzle me. If there's a Devil or a God, then there must be a God. In the event of Darkness Then there is Light.

You are One

The concept of Oneness reveals the unity of energy between Self in the Universe. Every person's energy field is a component of the energy of Universe. Our energy fields are in contact in a way with those of other people and animals, as well as nature and all objects that surround us. We affect everything that surrounds us, and we are influenced by everything.

While it may appear to be an original New Age concept, it's not. Oneness has been a concept that has been understood and practiced for centuries. In the ancient Pagan belief, "I am One" is a reference to "I I am Sun," "I am the tree,"" "I am light,"" "I am air,"" "I am fire,"" "I am love,"" "I am one with my neighbour," etc. Whatever you can think of you're one with. By thinking about it, you're already exchanging energy with it.

Imagine the trunk of a tree. The trunk of the tree is God or Universe If you want. Every leaf is a human. Although each leaf is an individual self-contained entity, it's also component of the trees. Leaves get essential nutrients through the trees, and return by absorbing solar energy and the energy of the air. If one leaf is infected there's a high possibility that the surrounding leaves are susceptible to the illness.

One person could infect the rest of humanity with negative energy. One person is also able to help others heal. Because Energy.

Energy

The universe is energy. Energy is not made, and it is not a thing that disappears. It simply transforms and moves. Energy is just that simple. It's like God. I am who I am. Energy is what binds atoms that moves air, and how we believe. Every single process is energy. Every thought is energy.

However, God is also everywhere. Does it mean that energy equals God? Partially, yes. Fully? It is impossible to say. Human brains aren't very advanced. What we have learned about the Universe is like a drop of water that is in the ocean.

Where does the human body get its energy? Food. Where is the energy going? It is through activities like walking or talking about food, thinking and sleeping, stressing out and so on. Every thought and every action is a move in a different direction and changes energy. How and where? The answer is dependent on one's own unconscious.

Quantum mechanics proves that each particle is a "information wave" that moves through the particle and guides it. A large number of these particles make the energy field.

Every emotion and thought is unique and has its own frequency. Positive thoughts have high frequency, while negative thoughts are lower.

Similar to emotions. It's the same with emotions. It's a spectrum. However, the degree of high you want to go, or how low, and the place in between is completely up to you.

Every human has an individual energy field, large or tiny. Aura, anyone?

We share energy with everyone and everything that surrounds us each day of our conscious and subconscious existence. If there is brain activity, we are One.

Question What is the reason I should keep my plans and ideas private?

If you discuss your thoughts with other people, there's an exchange of energy. You contribute the energy you have them, and they return an amount of energy back to them. The words you speak are energy. There's a possibility that they'll give your negative energies in form doubts. They could tell you about ways your plan might be delayed or hindered. Are you really in need of that negative feedback? Even if someone appears to be positive on the outside How do you tell if they're not snarky or jealous in their inner self?

If you are in contact with people whether through thoughts, words, or writing - you must be mindful of the energy you share and how much energy you are receiving. There are many people who would like your possessions, and not only in the physical sense, but also in the energy. They'll steal your strengths and then dump on you the negatives. Most of the time, they don't even realize the extent of their actions. It's part of their DNA. They aren't sure how to live a different life. There are people who release their negative energy for motives. Certain protection spells will protect you from this type of negativity.

"Stealing" magicks are extremely popular within dark magic. They are known as "kradnik." Be true your distance and using powerful protection spells can help you keep away those who would like your possessions and fortune, as well as your attractive appearance and love life.

Chapter 3: Spell Crafting

However, I'm going to go through the basic guidelines for crafting spells and rituals of magic.

In my daily witching rituals, I employ ancient Slavic rituals and spells which have been written down in Cyrillic. In rituals, I say words in the same way as they were written. Lucky for me, I was born into a storied Pagan bloodline, and was taught the art of reading Cyrillic. When I come up with new spells, I employ the old Cyrillic language. Habit.

A majority of the time I don't rely on old rituals in their original forms altering them to meet my specific situation and the end goal I'd like to accomplish. This is where my magical abilities come out. When I am grounded and am in a trance state, the words begin flooding. In some way, rhymes and words in Cyrillic appear in my mind, and these rhymes speak to exactly how I feel and what require. I note them down whenever I am able.

I would like you to not apply the exact examples provided within this publication. It's not because I'm lazy, but because words are important. The order in which words are used is important. These aren't even complete spells, but just pieces to help you understand how spells perform. Each spell needs to be carefully planned and written to meet your requirements and the situation.

Spell Power

Aspell will only prove as powerful as the witch that is performing it. A witch could throw salt in front of the doorway and get a huge protection for the house. Another witch can perform the same thing and leave only dirt on the floor.

Someone once told me that a pentacle must be drawn correctly otherwise it will not function. You could draw your pentacle as straight as you like. It's only about the Power you use to draw and the connection between your unconscious and your Soul.

If someone states that the spell isn't working for them, yet it does for other people it is because of oneself. Uncertainty, lack of energy or unclean energy can hinder a spell or cause unexpected results.

Writing Spells

Here are some useful strategies for casting a successful spell. Spells do not have to be written in rhymes, however they are simpler to remember and repetitious. However , they must be written in both past and current terms, and never in the future.

A good example of a properly written spelling:

Water took my sorrows,

I am full of happiness.

This is a common couplet for overcome an unpleasant experience. Even if you're the middle of the negative incident, the spell should be spoken as if it's already come to be. If you want to gain something, the spell must be phrased as if already possess it. It is not recommended to make use of the future tense when the crafting of spells as it can cause it to be placed on hold indefinitely. When will I feel full of happiness? Tomorrow? In an entire year? In the next year?

Repeat the spell repeatedly to experience the true meaning of a wish that is fulfilled. You can ask yourself: "If I had this already, how do I be feeling? Which would be my response? What thoughts would I make?" Find that feeling and then try to feel it. Feel the sensation in your body. This will help you generate the appropriate amount of energy to achieve that you're looking for.

A case of an incorrectly written spelling:

What isn't in my life?

I will not be able to control me.

This is supposed to provide safeguarding against external influences. In the beginning, we have the future past tense. What time will I be safe? I don't want it to happen next week, but I'm in need of it right now. From a the perspective of power the spell is of no protection and can result in unpredictable outcomes. We are part of an all-inclusive Universe and it will not consider negative assertions. What Power will be hearing is:

What's present in my daily life?

Will be in control of me.

This kind of curse, in the near future some aspect of your life will be able to influence you.

Key Lock, Key

This is a part that is specific for Slavic witches. Key the lock, the key and the tongue all are three essential elements in the creation of a spell. Every witch has her personal "key" along with a "lock" that were handed through generations. They are like passwords to log in.

If a witch performs an act of magic using a key and lock, the next witch won't be able to reverse the spell. It's protected. If another witch attempts to break your locked spell, you'll feel it and be able to retaliate. Only a strong witch can crack someone else's lock, however even then it's going to take enormous amounts of energy and the witch will end up with a weaker condition.

Sometimes, keys and locks are real objects along with spell words. Locks are locked during an ritual. If a witch decides to break her spells, she opens that lock.

These precautions are great to use protection spells. If you've secured protection spells for your family members and yourself there will be no harm to you.

"Key" refers to a particular phrase used at the beginning of the spell. "Lock" is spoken at the end of the spell to lock it into the position it was in. "Tongue" refers to the spell between.

Nothing to worry about

Don't attempt to tell Power how to perform its job. You'll get better results if tell Power only what you would like to see occur. If you'd like to go to Hawaii Don't solicit $5,000, instead, make an offer for the opportunity to go to Hawaii.

If you write down what you want to happen in a way, you are limiting your options. Your dream might not be fulfilled or achieved in a bizarre manner. The power of God has millions of other options to grant the things you desire. God has a way of working in mysterious ways.

Your task is to determine your ultimate target. What happens to it is not the issue. When you cast a spell you're out of control.

If your neighbors are bothering you Don't think of ways to get rid of them. You should seek peace and peaceful life at home. God determines how to get there, and He's a lot better than you at it.

Questions: I've handful of objects from the ritual that have been gifted to me. Some are brand new and others have been have been used. Is it risky to make use of them?

The principle is: every object that comes into your hands needs to be cleaned. This includes everything : clothing, kitchen equipment books, etc. This is crucial in the event that an item was previously utilized. Anything that are touched by humans are able to absorb some of their energy. This is a good thing but it could also be harmful. If you're in the wild, carrying an easy-to-use protection charm can protect you from the risk of harm immediately. When you return back home, a quick cleaning routine should be performed. It can be done using smoke or salted water.

Chapter 4: Rituals

Magical rituals are generally similar cleansing by grounding, making circles and calling upon spirits and elements. This is a straightforward formula. There are complex rituals that require a myriad of tools, but we won't get too far into them.

Below is an example the ritual used for charging an amulet using magic. Don't try to recreate the ritual; it's advanced magic that requires spirits, and should only be done by a teacher.

1. Find a suitable place to perform the ritual. Clear your mind. Take a break for a moment in meditation. Clean the room using rosemary, thyme, or sage or lighting incense. Set the symbols that represent the various elements onto the altar you've constructed. Create a candle to honor the God of the Universe.

2. Declare the goal of the ritual.

3. Cast an arc. (Cleansing, grounding , and casting the circle are discussed in the next chapters.)

4. Invite the God of your circle, and then burn the candle for her. Example: "I invoke the Forces of God Mars. I invite you to join my circle. Bring me power."

5. Take a moment to sit in a peaceful state. Experience the control of the forces that are Divine. Feel the way they fill you.

6. Place the amulet in your palms and carry it to the incense that is burning (or plants). Speak, "Powerful spirits of Air Make this amulet holy give it your power, to ensure that it (announce the purpose here, for instance: so that it can protect me). Let it be just as that is the way the way it should be." On top of the flame of the candle, say "Powerful Spirits of Fire Infuse this amulet with sanctity and give it your power to ensure it (state your purpose is able to achieve your goal). Let it be as that is." Set the amulet on symbolize the Earth (stones or salt and earth). Speak, "Powerful spirits of the Earth to make this amulet holy, and give the power to... It will be what that it will be." Over an oblong bowl of Water In a bowl of water, say (and add a little the water), "Powerful spirits of Water In sanctifying this amulet Give it your power to ensure that it (state your intention in this

section). Let it be as that is." Set the amulet in the middle of your altar, or hang it from the ceiling in the center of an open flame. Be aware of the power of the Four Elements will fill the amulet up with energy. Speak, "This amulet is sanctified by the Forces of the Four Elements with the blessing of Mars. Truly."

7. Rejoice in to the summoned Powers. If necessary, make a sacrifice.

8. Closing the magic circle, and clean.

It is not necessary for every activity to be performed as a full ritual of magic. If you're not asking for any gods or elements There is no need to make the formation of a circle. Sometimes you'll be able to look in the mirror, say one quick omorochka and you'll be off. (Omorochka is explained within this text.)

Rituals are routine actions. What is the best way to learn? Through repetition. Each ritual is intended to write or add on the unconscious mind.

Do you apply a cream on your face every day? This is a tradition and must be accompanied with a proper beauty rhyme.

If you water your the plants, play a short rhyme for each plant.

When there's a repeating exercise, it's best carefully planned with a rhyme spells to increase the effectiveness of the activity.

Magic crafting spells is a common routine. I'm guessing that you have a location that you have set up. Your ritual starts by doing the same thing every time cleansing: you wash the area, you ground, and you make circles. Certain routines put you into a safe and familiar state. They open your subconscious to suggestions, such as an hypnosis. Keep in mind that your Spirit receives information from your subconscious not from your conscious mind.

Cleaning

Rituals performed in nature require only a little cleansing, but it's important to wash the ritual when it is carried out inside a home. People who live in the area have a tendency to accumulate negative energy.

To cleanse, you'll require an instrument of witchcraft, such as the magic broom. There is no need to rub the floor using the broom. But, when you are you are working, think you're cleaning away any negative thoughts.

Another method of cleansing the sacred space can be to sprinkle salt in a pure form as well as mixed in with other herbs, or resins. You can make use of thyme incense, rosemary, copal (modern or fossil tree resin) or sage, as well as the dragon's blood (red resin from the dragon tree). It is also possible to make use of salt water.

Perform a musical instrument using the 4/4 rhythm as you move clockwise around. Burn aromas and plants with cleansing properties like frankincense myrrh and sage, as well as rosemary, and thyme in combination or on their own.

Grounding

The practice of grounding is among the most essential elements of a magical ritual. Another term used to describe the practice is called meditation. It's the time when all external distractions disappears when your mind isn't thinking about the future, present, or past. The world shrinks to fit into your magical circle.

Like regular meditation, shut your eyes and begin by focusing on your body. Let go of tension. Focus on breathing and, most importantly, the breath gaps. In those gaps, there are Nothingness or the unobserved. Being in Nothingness is a peaceful, tranquil experience. It is in this place that everything occurs. It's the only place that free particles can exist without any energy. You, now, is using energy to create.

Herbs, candles and crystals

Awitch does not use her own energy to create magic. Ever. The constant depletion of your energy can lead to illness and premature old age.

This is why you've got your tiny helpers - crystals herbs, candles and what else you like. Each item has its own distinct qualities which you can draw energy from. Find out what works best for you and then use it to serve your needs most effectively. Of course every object must be cleaned prior to use during an ritual.

Note: Herbs must be grown locally, and candles must be constructed with genuine wax and not paraffin. The best candles are long thin candles used in church. Candles must be completely burning during a ceremony. A candle that is blow-out signifies that you have renounced an oath. If it accidentally goes out, the ceremony must be re-run.

In my experience I have found that rituals performed outdoors, in nature, and with bare feet on the floor yield the most effective results. Earth itself is a gigantic battery of infinite energy.

Casting the Circle

Amagic circle is created to keep something inside or out. If you're looking to protect yourself, you can cast a protection circle to keep negative energy out. For rituals that involve magic the circle is a powerful tool that protects you from energy while also protecting yourself from harmful energy from outside.

When you are a beginner at drawing, you'll draw circles in the dirt. You can make use of any object to make a circle for example, a rope or flowers. The circle must be large enough to allow just a few steps within. The most experienced witches draw circles mentally. My circle is always a sphere filled with flames.

Be sure to have everything you require before casting your magical circle. The process of opening and closing to let in and out is draining your energy.

When your circle is shut After the circle is closed, you can summon spirits and elements, in case you need to. It is important to note that different witchcraft traditions contain different arrangements for elements. I have observed rituals where Earth and Water are reversed in their placement.

Spirits

Please be careful not to summon spirits without having a mentor during the ritual. It's hard for a novice witch to manage spirits. It takes a lot of practice and a strong connection with Power.

Spiritual beings of The Higher World are not easy to summon as your frequency of energy has to match the frequency of theirs. That means you must be clear of doubt and negativity.

Spirits from spirits from the Lower World come easily because people have a lot of doubts and thoughts. In addition, once the doorway towards The Lower World is open, it's not only the spirit you've requested which is likely to come through Some others could get through, too. You won't even be aware of the number or what to do with the other spirits. If you shut the door and return the item that was referred to as and all the extras remain and create chaos on your life and the lives of those surrounding you.

I am convinced that our world is currently in an awful state due to the fact that magic is widely practiced without thinking and with carelessness. The people are unaware of the negative effects they can bring to the world through their actions.

As a kid I was taught spirit protection. Since the time, not a single spirit has harmed the family or me. The spirits of the higher World are present when I ask them. The lower spirits are a far cry. People frequently say that they feel calm when they are near me. They refer to it as "presence." It's because when people are in the energy of my body, my boundary protections are able to block their negative energy and keep evil spirits out. After I've left the energy field is restored.

I've been to all kinds of "haunted" locations. Yawn. While the rest of the world was frightened, looking and hearing what, regardless of the location, I was calm and peaceful.

I do not call on Spirits that come from The Lower World during magic rituals even when I'm in the magic circle and all of my personal security measures are off. This is since I'm not wanting my power to be contaminated. I'm trying to maintain it as high as is possible.

Question: How do find out if a person is haunted by spirits?

Inform them that you believe they're possessed, and observe their reactions. If they're hostile in denial, then there's a high probability that they are possessed. Also, you can go through the prayers priests make to remove evil spirits. Watch their reactions. Don't attempt to exorcise spirits on your own as you'll get yourself into trouble. Most lower-level spirits respond strongly to attempts to eliminate them from a person. Higher-level spirits, generally are not possessed by humans.

Vacuum Effect

The Law of Vacuum states that when you take something away the space that is created creates the form of a vacuum and immediately will take in something. The exact nature of that will depend on you. If you don't act it will be filled with the same energy that was eliminated. If you take out undesirable stuff, but don't immediately replace it with positive the vacuum will be filled by the old.

Water took my sorrows,

I am full of happiness.

It can be a good example for what can be done with flowing water, such as an aquifer. Water is an excellent element to cleanse and renew. Give your burdens to water , and instantly make a vacuum full of happiness. Don't be concerned about where your negative energy might be deposited. Earth as well as Earth will take the responsibility. Make sure to touch the running water in your rituals, however it's necessary for exchange of energy.

What do you do if you are in an urban area? When cleansing spells are being performed my advice, as well as the way I was taught is to always place negative energy into the object and then use a fire to burn it. It could be the cut hair you cut after having a haircut. It could be a piece of rope after you've cut your rope. It could be something that expresses your grievances.

Do you remember that law of energy? It doesn't just vanish and disappear, it transforms. If you simply speak about what you would like to eliminate Words matter as they represent energy what happens to it? Everything bad will go somewhere, most likely within your life. If you burn it, but fire converts it into energy that is heat. Ta-dah, it's gone. Now, fill the empty space with your thoughts and emotions about something you'd like to have.

For the love of God Do not place your negative thoughts into a container and discard it. That's dark magic.

You don't ever know what you'll get when you remove any negative obstacle. It could be something exciting and thrilling and far more than you imagined. It depends on the amount of the unneeded energy was eliminated, and the type of energy you got instead.

Even modern psychology has picked on old witchcraft practices. We've all heard of writing down your negative thoughts and burning the paper. Hello! White witches are here! We've been doing this for many centuries! But, modern psychology has not taken the second step: once you feel that sense of relief, you need immediately communicate, imagine or write down what you would like to achieve or take place. In the event that you don't, your relief could quickly turn to disappointment.

Chapter 5: Dark Witchcraft

Dark witchcraft is far more powerful than white. Evil is always more powerful than Good. However, evil is also self-destructive.

Darkness stems from basic emotions - fear, anger and shame. The quality of life comes from awareness. it's secondary to the fundamental emotions. Dark magic is extremely dangerous and prohibited, which is why it's attracted to certain types of people.

It's hard for a novice witch to discern whether a ritual is either white or dark. The first thing you need to be asking is "Is the ritual in violation of someone's wishes?" If there is no third party or a second and it's an individual witch who is doing her own thing and her own purposes, then you're in the sure. If there's another person in the picture, you must be granted permission by that person. Same applies to the third party.

If there's biological substance involved, like blood hair, fingernails or nails, etc. - it's dark magic. The lower beings are drawn to flesh of humans. They attach themselves to and transmit the power of the person.

Graveyard rituals , or any other objects found in a graveyard or other graves are dark magic. Death and necromancy are gateways into The Lower World.

Rituals that involve spirit guides from The Lower World: please be extremely cautious when performing rituals that invoke spirits. Study the spirit you would like to summon. Most of the time the moment a doorway to another realm is opened there is an opportunity for undiscovered spirits to slip through.

There's a trick that is used by dark witches. They'll convince you that they possess a special power with no negative effects. All you have to do is simply say, "I agree." You should be scared. Feel very terrified.

And then there are "grey" witches. They say they use dark and white magic, and double-dipping. Nobody can be a servant to two masters. Go through your Bible.

Curses

Acurse is a spell that carries negative energy and is meant to hurt the victim. Dark magic.

It is difficult to remove curses. They're usually locked and are only able to be lifted through the witch that put the curse. Witches may also place "guards" alongside the lock. These guards are spirits of lower realms, or lower levels of The Lower World.

Only way to avoid being cursed is to put the best protection available.

Victims may try to ease adverse effects by increasing energy levels of their personal energy field. A third witch can assist to make the curse bearable. Do you remember Sleeping Beauty, where a dark witch is able to cast a death curse, while a witch of white transforms it into a sleeping curse? Similar to the one in that.

Cemetery

Let's get this straight that only dark witches can have rituals at cemeteries, or make use of objects that are found in cemeteries. White witches visit cemeteries to grieve loved ones, that's it.

Cemeteries are places of low-frequency energy. The suffocation of the dead within a small space, the emotional pain of the pain and anxiety that people feel when they visit the cemetery, all of this creates a unique cemetery aura. Naturally, this aura is felt by everything in it, be it people who are dead, or the deceased, or any items found in graveyards.

In the dictionary of witches, there is a concept as an active , living grave. Near graves, plants flourish. Insect and animal activity is high. Most often, there are anthracites within the vicinity.

If you notice signs of a graveyard that's active it could mean that rituals of magic are frequently performed in this location. The dark witches "bind" deceased souls to the mortal world to gain their energy. This means that the soul is not able to rest and is able to continue its journey in the realm of the living.

If you see objects in a grave you didn't bring, don't be able to touch it. On the burial, a dark witch might leave an "ransom" in the name of the person who died, a gift which she offers to show her gratitude. It could be anything: money, dolls or doll, a bottle of liquor or the deck of cards, or a flower arrangement. It's essential to arrange an oath at church to pray to honor the soul of your beloved one.

Cemetery dirt is an everyday item used in the dark arts, utilized predominantly to cast death curses and love spells. The significance of graveyard dirt should be evident - it's dead energy which obliterates and blocks all other forms of energy.

It's often said that I'm mistaken about witches' practices at cemeteries. They say that it's not "dark" in the practice, and that it's merely appealing to the gods. They're not deities that come from The Higher World; those are gods of Death. They say they have a lower spirit or the

Spirit of the Dead to an individual as a way to safeguard them. Does this mean that they create the person to a negative energy field to shield themselves from negative energy? What sense would that make? If you're honest, that's ignorant. at worst it's malicious.

A dark witch might say that she performs rituals to gain wealth and grants wishes. Selling souls for money, anyone?

Love spells are among the most harmful. A spirit of the dead can be employed to either remove an opponent or keep the victim close to the solicitor against their desire. If you are able to name that love, you are able to keep it.

Questions: Does it legal to keep dirt out of an area of burial in the living spaces?

Under no circumstances! Ever! The energy of the grave is energy that has died and will draw your energy source to bring about illness or even death.

Love Spells

The love spell is dark magic. If someone claims that there are no negative effects, they're lying.

Dark magic can force victims to be drawn against their wishes. White magic can open the way for lawyers to locate the most suitable person.

Easy spells are made by using the photo of a victim. More complex spells rely on dolls or blood (voodoo dolls). Some even make use of graveyard dirt or spirits from the Lower World.

At the point that someone's family or a victim recognize that something is not right it is often already on the road to self-destruction.

Although a victim is unable to break the magic connection, the victim thinks that their partner is the primary source of the blame for their plight of being. The retribution will manifest as anger and/or addiction.

Some of the strongest love spells are performed with menstrual blood. This kind of spell is also brutal. This isn't even a ritual it's the curse. Menstrual blood that is cursed can make an innocent man old and continue to be an ongoing curse for generations. A person who suffers from the condition may be unstable and require medical assistance or perhaps hospitalization.

A woman who is soliciting her blood collected to a witch who performs an act of worship. The enhanced blood can later be added to drinks, food and even perfumes, clothing or photographs. The blood may be sprayed onto dolls using the victim's biological material such as hair.

The blood of a man brings out the animal-like nature in males. These are lower-level instincts, such as desire for sexual satisfaction. These urges aren't distant from violence and aggression. The aim of the victim will be to control the woman using any methods. He will not be stopped by anything.

As as a rollback (more on rollbacks in the future) to this type of dark magic the woman who was a victim of blood magic could receive a crown of celibacy worn on her and could also be passed on to future generations as a curse.

The most harmful spells for love are made using dirt that is taken out of the tombstones an unrighteous person. It binds a Lower Spirit on the person who is being abused.

Every person involved in the love spell is affected. If there's a protection spell placed on an target, then the spell caster could be hit with a rollback, perhaps with negative energy.

The removal of a love spell can be complicated, but not impossible. It should be performed by a qualified witch only. If you are locked in love by a new witch, it could be a disaster for the victim. An experienced witch will likely perform the spell in phases. Start by removing the lock, and then do the cleaning.

Selling and buying Souls

It's not an enchanting fairytale. Let's look at the reasons the reason behind the practice of purchasing souls. The Higher and Lower Worlds are in constant conflict. It's more or less Lower World constantly agitates Higher World due to the fact that Higher World is closer to God and is more energetic. It's the Middle World of humanity is the battlefield. The main motivation behind the battle is energy. Whoever has greater energy prevails. The fuel for that energy is the feelings that are that are generated through our inner soul.

Souls are the bridge between our minds and Spirit. It is due to our souls we can tell right from wrong, good from bad. Our souls initially belonged to God however, we were granted free will. The way we use our souls in our lives is completely up to us.

Who is the one who buys souls? Lucifer Of course. He is not the only one, but through others who are controlled by a lesser spirit. What's the cost? It depends on the "soul to be sold."

Selling your soul can be done, though it is difficult. There aren't all souls available to be sold. Certain souls are not a good choice for buyers. The more pure and positive a person's soul is, the greater the cost. Sinners' souls are of little worth to the lower World.

Souls always in a negative mood that is sad, angry or jealous, naive and lonely - already have a tendency to match their energies to their counterparts in Lower World; there's no requirement to pay a steep cost for them. However, they are still able to do the bidding of the Devil.

If a soul that is positive changes the energy of its body to negative it's an enormous victory for the lower World and the negative energy field expands.

Concerning the transaction: A seller must break off the ties to any religionand then pledge to follow The Power of Darkness. The seller will receive the amount provided. Then, the lower beings appear and let"the "sold human" perform whatever needs to do within the Middle World. It's mostly to attract new souls.

Of course, anyone willing to sell their souls to Devil receives what they desire. It is usually material wealth such as property or money. Sometimes, it's about being well-behaved, loved, or to be successful. A lot of people gain influence and power. This is why there are millions of billionaires, politicians and others selling their hearts.

In our daily lives, everything is sold and bought. The human soul is not an exception. There are countless stories of people selling their lives to the Devil at a cost that included legendary historical figures as well as our influential contemporary counterparts.

There is no way to come to this Dark side. The Dark energy affects people's perceptions. They perceive and experience differently. The people living in the Dark side aren't able to even contemplate moving to the Light because it's physically difficult.

How can you tell whether you've been scammed to sell your soul? If, during a magical ritual, you are asked to respond, "I agree," and that's all it takes.

Fake psychics

They are easy to identify. If you see someone advertising supernatural services, it's probably a scam. It's most likely a direct fraud, however, it could be a weak psychic, who has relatives who had abilities, but nature didn't pick this one. Sometimes, it's a person who's mentally unstable.

Whatever, if you come across advertisements, stay away.

The people who are connected to the power (through Spirit) - we're talking witches here . They don't have to promote. They either do not for other people or have enough solicitors through words of mouth that keep their hands active. Witches are also able to bring cash into their lives with no work.

Important note: If you have a psychic who has offered to cast an love spell for you and you believe that it's not a scam it's probably a dark wizard. There are consequences.

It is important to stress this that Finding a white witch who will cast a spell on you is not likely. There are very few witches who do magic for money.

Fake psychics usually write books and instruct on magic. It is difficult to imagine the damage the teachings of fake psychics cause.

Rollback

There are always risks associated with the use of magic, particularly dark magic.

Rollback occurs when your spell isn't recognized by the recipient. The spell generates the energy field. The energy field is directed at a specific target. If the target you want to reach rejects the energy, it won't disappear, it goes back its sender.

There are two main reasons spells are not accepted. The first is due to the subconscious. Humans have limits in their minds that are subconscious. Go through the "Subconscious" section of this book to find out more. If a spell fails to reach the target's subconscious line the spell is rejected.

Another reason spells are not accepted is due to protection spells. They cause a much more severe rollback. Some witches use simple protection spells. This is a mirror effect that mirrors back what was cast. Others witches, including me typically include "key as well as lock" to spells of protection. The "lock" portion contains an encapsulation that weakens the energy of the sender. The effect of this destabilization on the sender's energy is unclear because it is controlled by Power. Thus, a spell that is malicious can be a boomerang for the person casting it by generating more negative energy due to the spell of protection. This is negative for witches casting the spell on someone secured.

Some rollbacks are not bad, but. Example: I'd like to make a friend feel better and so I cast an omen for her to take her to Hawaii for one week. Surprise! My friend doesn't believe in magic, and does not have any protection therefore the spell must be effective. But, for reasons I am not aware of my friend is averse to Hawaii. Thus, the spell bounces for me and then I am able to enjoy an entire week under the Hawaiian sun.

It's clearly a fictitious scene, yet it demonstrates the way The Golden Rule works. Do to others what you would want them to do to you! If you are casting spells the first thing you should ask yourself is include: "Would I be OK should this spell be done by me?"

Question: The plants in my home have were dead within a few days. What's happening?

This could be cause for serious concerns. If all the plants were similar that could indicate an natural disease. However, the majority of species aren't able to infect one another. Roses can be infected by other roses but they aren't able to cause a gardenia to become sick. The ground may be affected as well. However, if you find multiple plants dying both inside and out there is a problem.

Plants respond to both the energy of positive and negative. It is possible that someone in your home has negative energy. Have you had an emotional time? Sadness? Aggression? Depression? That's the most obvious solution.

I've seen a lot of people with negative energy that have beautiful gardens. They were just similar to that. There was never a sudden shift of their energy. The plants had adapted to their needs.

Plants dying this way may be the first indication of an evil spell In this case, it is imperative to cleanse your home immediately. Your home and the land must be cleaned first. It is then possible to determine the presence of negative energy in the area. It is easy to do this using a candle, which is described in the following book.

Chapter 6: Daily Practice

Witches are not magical genie. She doesn't simply snap her fingers and let things happen according to her wishes. Witches train daily. They study books and keep journals. They usually fail. But, more importantly, they strive to improve themselves constantly.

Protection

There are a myriad of rituals and protection spells that can be used in each circumstance. In this article, I will explain the most basic method was taught to us as we were young. It's known as "the Wall."

If you meet someone who you don't like, create an imaginary wall between yourself and the person. It could be any type of wall: block, concrete, or light It doesn't matter. It's always lit by fire because my people worship the ancient God of the Sun. My magic is based on either fire or light but you could also construct an ice wall in case you want. If you have to talk to someone you want to talk to, it must appear as if they're in a glassy haze that you cannot hear or see them.

After that, perform the ritual of putting your wall in a circles around yourself. In reality, it's not a circle; it's an circle. It's like in an inflated bubble, or in the case of me, inside the ball of fire. Another fantastic one is the mirror circle. It mirrors what's visible from the outside and reflect it back.

There's a trick to it, however. When performing a ritual, you must specify that you want to allow all good things through and ward off all negative things. Higher frequency energy must be able to move through. Additionally, when performing a ritual avoid the normal circle casting as it is not advisable to have two circles surrounding you. Don't shut the circle. You do not want to close your circle of protection along with your ritual circle. Make sure to keep your mind fresh and refresh your protective spell each day. Each day, imagine your circle around you.

The lock and key can be used as an additional security layer for your security circle. It's not necessary, but it's beneficial. There are many strong dark witches that have the ability to break the protection spells. The lock will disable them for a time. It will make you feel as if you're under attack. However, lock and key will allow you to get your house protected. The dark witches who cast down protection spells work in stages, removing lock on one day, and protect next day, and they can do as they like.

How do you determine whether you're being targeted? If you suddenly experience uncontrollable thoughts of fear or despair and these feelings are not typical for you, it could be that you are being targeted.

I'm not going to go into the specifics of the ritual for protection as this is a introductory guide, and not an exhaustive reference to practice magic. As a novice witch, you'll need to work on your wall-building skills.

I'm asking: What's your strongest security I can obtain?

You'll be safe from harm if always wear a necklace of the cross handed to you during your baptism. If your cross gets lost and you want to replace it, you can purchase an alternative, but it should be cleansed by holy water. Protection spells are able to be placed on the cross and must be replaced as required. White magic and holy water are not in conflict. White magic is basically a plea to Higher Power that is the power of God.

If you suspect that you've got an outbreak of "evil eye" happening Take a bath (it's flowing water, after all) and pray for protection.

Question Do I have the ability to create my own holy water?

Yes holy water is able to be prepared at home using either salt or the silver cross. I have both. The most basic ritual is purifying the water and blessing. The water can do the trick, but it's not as powerful than Epiphany water.

In Orthodox custom, on Epiphany the 19th of January, water blessed is believed to possess special power. Regular believers and white witches can take a dip in the blessed river water to honor Jesus' baptism. Jesus Christ. Water that has been blessed by the Holy Spirit from springs is collected into Jars and stored throughout the duration of the year, up to the next Epiphany.

Question: How do I determine if the home has negative energy?

Make a candle white and then walk around the house clockwise. Stop at every corner. Check if and where the flame begins to explode and smoking. These are areas of negative energy.

Cutting Hair

If I inform people that I don't go to a hairdresser with the exception of Olga I'm sure they'll think I'm insane. I'm convinced that they're crazy.

Hair's magical power is known for quite a while. Hair is not just a way to enhance the appearance, but it can also have a significant impact on its owner's their health as well as career, and even social life. So, it is important to take care of your hair and be careful not to damage it, or you could be putting yourself in danger too.

If you've made the decision to get hair cut, the stylist should be selected with care as the person cutting your hair is going to be having an energetic influence on your. Select the appropriate day by focusing upon the moon's cycle. If you'd like your hair to expand faster after cutting it the hair, do it at the time that the moon is fresh. If you wish for your hair to alter its characteristics - for instance to help calm those "naughty" ones you must visit the hair salon on the night of the waning moon. A moon that is waning will help strengthen hair's roots, and will slow down its loss in speed.

What is not permitted is to cut your hair on the satanic lunar day (9 15 and 23 and 29 as per the lunar calendar) or on days of lunar or solar eclipses. Cuts on these days could make you feeling sick, or as people were used to say in the past, "cut off from your memories and thoughts."

Another important rule Do not cut your hair yourself. Since cutting your hair affects your energy field and that of the person who is cutting it so you'll be able to be impacted by it. The only thing to consider is the effect it will have. Whatever the strength of one is, it is extremely difficult to correct the deformations that occur to your own energy field.

Hair that has been cut, and even hair that remains on the comb is ideal to burn or put in a septic tank, to ensure that you don't use up the energy stored in it. Additionally, you don't want to let your energy accumulated to be misused against you.

Omorochka

Omorochka refers to "to be fooled." This is a short-term spell that is designed to alter the perception of people around you. Beware! A thin line divides the magic of white from that of dark.

Sometimes you'd like to be seen. Sometimes, you don't. Based on your requirements, omorochka can cause others to perceive you in a different way. Invisibility cloaks are an effective Omorochka.

If you're planning to go to the party and you'd like to get to be the center of attention, perform Omorochka before leaving the home. Men will be over you like you're the most beautiful girl on the planet. There will be no other women. Who wouldn't like an increase in confidence? Some witches are able to totally change their appearance.

There are two methods to get the omorochka effect. One is to alter your self-generated energy field. The second is to alter others minds. However, the other can be described as dark magic. What is the different? It's in the language.

Here's one. Pick a plant that is dried and say:

When this plant dried as it did, so do all men and suffer, without my focus.

This is clearly a violation of this law. Law of Free Will. It's dark magic.

Another illustration:

I praise myself

Today, at this hour,

All hours throughout the day,

To the crowd of people

The most gorgeous of all

The most beautiful of all, and the most dearest,

More bright than the moon and more bright than the sun...

This scenario alters the energy field surrounding witches, making them appear different from other. It's not a problem.

Omorochka can be performed for as many times as you like, but you must beware: your mask is removed eventually, but it isn't clear the exact time. The strength and length of the spell is dependent solely on your.

Important note: If you're planning to start a romantic relationship, do not make use of omorochka in any way. Your partner will know your real self at some time. Beginning a relationship by telling the intention of lying is never a good idea.

Magical objects

Every object is an object of magic. Every object has energy. certain types more, others less. Everything around us possess qualities and features that can be either organic or created by humans. Because of these characteristics they may exhibit diverse effects on other objects. The effects could be positive or negative.

If you're looking to guard your home from harm Make a beautiful wreath using your hands. Flowers, seeds, herbs and pins are required in your wreath. (Pins should be hidden so that they are not visible.)

The keys to your car and home keys are amulets of protection. Your car should be equipped with an amulet that is hung in the rear view mirror. If properly activated and charged, the magical object will increase the strength of your security. To charge an device with energy, it is have to carry out a particular ritual or visualize it in your mind when you have enough experience.

There are witches that eliminate their negative energy by making it into small objects and then throwing them on the streets which random people are able to grab them. I have been working hard to improve my routine of not grabbing coins. It's a good thing that they're nearly gone. It's in my DNA now that anything I get my hands on could spell the curse.

The most frequent practice of Dark witches to do is stick curses or negative energy on a sewing pin, and then put it on a person's clothingor furniture during a visit to someone's home. It's nearly impossible to find and it can remain for years, causing havoc within people's lives.

The most common rule is that when you discover a small , sharp or shiny object in your home or vehicle, or even clothing such as an object that shouldn't be there, it's an indication for massive cleansing and casting on protection spells. As an example, we've not ever used coins in a long time. If I discover an unaccounted for coin in my pocket I go into an uncontrollable anxiety. I then clean it thoroughly and renew my security.

Large Gatherings

This isn't a warning but rather a suggestion for consideration. There are individuals and lower beings in our world who understand how to harness and convert energy in a massive way. To gather that huge amount of energy into one location the only thing you need to do is to get a large number of people and force them to do the same thing and preferably, something that is emotional. A greater number of people and more emotions means more energy is flowing out. Magic is more effective in covens. Doesn't it?

New Year's Eve, sporting celebrations and religious gatherings are great examples of hot spots for energy. These events were planned to serve this purpose way long ago in the past. Created by who? by the most powerful people on the planet. They used these spikes in energy to further their own goals.

"But I'm feeling energized by these occasions!" you say. You are an energy-hungry person, which is not the case for the majority of people who feel exhausted and exhausted. Feel free to go to these kinds of occasions to replenish your energy. For those who experience fatigue loss after attending massive gatherings, I'm saying you should stop attending. I'm simply asking that you make an educated decision.

Fasting and Meat

Fasting prior to rituals is recommended to get clean energy. Food is what we eat in the end.

However, that doesn't mean a completely abstinence from food. It's about eating clean. Clean food is the closest to its natural state as is possible. There is no processing. Organic vegetables, organic fruits and homemade breads are your best bets.

It is widely practiced by dark witches to stay away from food for three days prior to the important ceremony. An extended state of hunger triggers basic instincts in human beings. These are the lower-level instincts which can lead to low spirits.

Meat doesn't fall into"the "clean" food group even if it's organic pasture-raised what. Modern farms are horrifying. Meat isn't just packed with chemicals, but it's also full of disease and suffering. Take a look at a piece meat and contemplate its past as a wild animal living in cramped surroundings far from sun. This creature was sick, and was treated with a variety of drugs. It was given hormones to help growth and endured daily discomfort for the rest of its existence. Then , it was killed.

The power of the suffering and pain is contained present in the piece of meat that is in your face. When you eat it, it transforms into your energy. Consuming meat is eating fear, pain and death. This energy will manifest in the form of magic. Of course, this negative energy will be sucked out quickly enough by routine cleansing ceremonies.

I'm not telling you to cut down on eating meat. I'm just asking you to look at the origin. If the chickens were outside in peace and were slaughtered painlessly and painlessly, your energy remains free of any dirt. If you're planning your big event, avoid eating meat for the next 2-3 days before the event.

Relationships

It's hard for a witch involved in a romantic relationship since we'll be honest here Her power scares men. A lot of witches are drawn towards the darker side. It's scary for everyone and not just men.

In the past, witches were never married. If they get married they usually have a disastrous end.

Does this mean that there's no reason to try? Absolutely not. Everyone attempts and a romantic relationship is possible even for the white witch.

We're in a different century. People are getting more open and spiritual, not only religious. Witchcraft isn't only black magic anymore. White witches are now accepted. Paganism is a recognised faith in the United States. Your best option is to locate someone willing to discuss your beliefs. Don't try to conceal what you're like. This will not be a good thing.

The most effective relationship would be between the two. However, witches are not common. The males aren't as observant or connected to their own inner self or Spirit as women are. Finding a good witcher could be difficult.

What is an witch to do to find a lover? She needs to eliminate self-destructing blocks. The Universe is abundant. There are numerous chances to get all we want every second of the day. Why don't we achieve it? Because we're afflicted with negative mental blockages. We don't always notice God-ordained opportunities, or we turn them away in our subconscious.

A lot of witches are involved in relationships that are not good. Being a witch implies that you be connected to Power. This does not mean witches have their shit together.

Question: If I am unable to make use of a love spell or omorochka spell, then how can I find someone to be my person to be my partner?

In this case, we presume that you are not suffering from curses such as the crown of celibacy , or the loneliness curse. They are curses that when discovered, should be handled by a skilled witch.

The first step is to be clear: is it an individual you are looking for? or a general capability to attract a person? Solutions to your problems with love will always be within your unconscious. If you're with a person who's not available either married, or even engaged, your behaviour is unhealthy. Even if the person is single, but isn't interested in a romantic connection with you reliance on them could be an indication of neurotic dependence. You should seek help from a professional. In this case, using magic could only make the situation worse.

If you're not able to find a partner regardless of the reason there is a root cause. They are pushed away subconsciously. There isn't anyone else there. You can find plenty individuals who could be ideal for you. However, they seem to aren't interested in you. Why? What is it about your personality that makes you seem inaccessible or invisible? What fears, beliefs, and doubts do your have that influence your energetic field?

Begin by writing down any negative experience you've experienced in an intimate relationship. Begin at the beginning of your youth. What was your relationship to your parents? What was their relationship like? What was the impact on you? List all your complaints. Did you feel you were not appreciated or loved? This is the most frequent answer. You can take those negative feelings and go through a rope-cutting burning ritual. Attach a rope to your hands and candles. Be sure to express your emotions. Be patient and cry. Do it for hours if you like. Get rid of all the negative energy out of yourself and into the flame. When you're ready for saying goodbye Cut the rope and burn it.

When you are empty, thin as air, you can begin taking in positive thoughts. Consider "What do I need? What makes me happy? What would I like to see occur?" Write down your thoughts. Make a vision board , and create an attracting routine. Do you envision yourself in Paris in the spring? You wake up, and you drink coffee with your loved one on a balcony looking out across the slick Parisian streets? Are you hearing dulcet French voices in the air? Do you smell the buttery aroma of the croissants baked in the Boulangerie? Incorporate this energy into your job.

Here's a very close version of the ancient love spell that attracts women:

"Destined By the Power of God, each in a pair,

Enjoy joys and sorrows together Joy and sorrow,

My life is governed by the most savviest Laws,

Love is a constant part of my life.

I am happy and makes me happy for the person I love.

Who is fated for me.

(S)He arrives at me by the power of God.

It is."

It is possible that you will have to repeat this cleansing and renewal routine several times before you see results. It's all about how much your energy has been affected by the.

This is merely an illustration of how psychological blocks could be eliminated and replaced with positive thoughts. It is important to remember that you must identify the negative experiences that impact your life and then eliminate the energy. Perhaps you must apologize to your parents or others who hurt you. Perhaps you're angry. Perhaps it's fear. Find that demon , and take it out.

Question What's different between celibacy crown and the loneliness curse? What can I tell if have one, and which?

The fact that a woman's crown is celibacy does not prevent a victim from having children and relationships. However, marriage is not possible.

The curse of loneliness prevents the victim from engaging in any kind of relationship either social or romantic.

Both of these curses are inherited and both are performed by witches of the dark. Any other magician or white witch won't be able to eliminate the curse. A skilled witch will be able to perform the diagnostics to see whether a curse exists.

Do I have any magic spells to make me appear younger and more beautiful?

Of course. White and dark spells are both valid. Dark spells can help you get there fast, but they can cause future issues. White spells are more time-consuming but will provide you with lasting beauty and health.

White spells to improve beauty and health should be carried out regularly. Each waning moon is a time when the cleansing spell is performed that removes imperfections, negatives as well as signs of aging. It also can also remove lines or wrinkles. It is common for there to be not visible effects for a few days or even weeks. Then you'll see that the problem is gone. I've performed rituals with apples to get rid of moles.

Every time the moon waxes, there is a ritual to enhance beauty: well-groomed hair, clear skin and more. There are also full moon spells that promote health. There is no beauty or youth without excellent health.

There are also smaller routines that are commonplace, such as enhanced facial creams as well as milk baths. There is a small bar made of hard lotion which I cut into pieces, which I then transform into "magic erasers." Each time the item gets used up, it gradually takes away wrinkles.

It is essential to be surrounded by beautiful things. Potted flowers, which aren't cut, may be arranged inside the home. I love small, potted roses in the indoors. Every day , I participate in an energy exchange. I place a rose on my eyes, take a sniff, and then say, "As you are the most beautiful woman, I am the most beautiful of everyone." Be cautious with this specific spell however, people may think you are imperceptible and cold. If the plant dies which is often the case due to the energy I draw through it, then I purchase an entirely new one. I have a rose bush outside also, but they do not bloom throughout the year.

If you choose to opt for a cosmetic surgery A spell that is accompanied by it will assist you in getting more effective outcomes.

I am a living example of how beauty and health spells are effective. I'm getting close to my 50th birthday, and so far, I've never had an entire day suffering except for giving birth. I'm never sick, and I never experience discomfort within my body. I've never lost weight. I'm still carrying my 120-pound 17-year-old body. My skin's quality is higher than that of a 20-year-old. I do not wear foundation as it hides my "healthy look." I receive daily compliments and inquires about my secrets. Magic.

Money

After love spells Money spells are second most sought-after. The rule of thumb is to perform money-attracting spells in the waxing moon as well as debt-banishing spells on the waning of the moon. However, things can get complicated.

Let's make it clear The dark side may make you a lottery winner however it comes with a significant cost. Many lottery winners fail to pay off their debts within a couple of years, or even worse some have even died or watched their loved family members suffer.

White magic can open the way for you to get cash naturally. Cash-flows appear all over the place. Credit cards get paid. Debts get smaller. You've saved enough to take you to take your Hawaii vacation. But , somehow your overall picture remains the same. You're not swimming in cash. You need to plan your plan your budget. You are wondering why you're not receiving the much-needed break you need.

The reason is that your subconscious mind can sabotage your ability to think clearly. Recall your childhood. "We aren't wealthy." "Money doesn't appear on the tree." "We are a family that lives from one paycheck." "Rich individuals are not good." "Money has no value." "Money is filthy." Does all of that seem familiar? I'd guess yes.

You speak to your Spirit via your subconscious mind as well as your emotions. Your subconscious is the one who tells these stories of money-blocking to your spirit. It is possible that your "money energies" is stained by poverty.

What do Power get when it gets an inquiry for money? "Four thousands of dollars, and to help with poverty I'd like to request." Accepted.

Then I realized I was spending every penny I earn plus a bit more. It was excellent money even according to California standards. If I'd had won the lottery at the time I'd be featured on television as one of the failed winners. Most were.

I asked the Universe why I spend more than I should. After half an hour, I was browsing YouTube and the suggested film that was "About money." Then I watched it. One of the smart people on the video mentioned that I love the action and challenges more than I do. I find it boring to save It's like being a slave to my own. This was true but I was unsure what to do about it. I don't want to be without taking action and tackling the challenges.

I asked a second question to Universe and that clever person, in the final 2 minutes explained that I'll earn enough money to meet all of my needs if my earnings are linked to my passion.

After some more exploring, I came up with an idea. It was revealed that although I was in a good and well-paying work, it an employment opportunity which I didn't like. My negative feelings towards the job, and my anxiety about losing it, were the main financial blockages. Did you notice that phrase "losing" within the preceding sentence? It was. Losing it. Money is lost! Whatever amount I earn I'd be losing everything! The light bulb!

Power offered me money I had asked for, but quickly revoked it because I was afraid of losing my enthusiasm.

I wanted to eliminate my anxiety about losing my job and earning money. This was the first step. Do you remember the effect of vacuum? I was in need of something to replenish the lost energy. Memory flashback: "... income tied to my passion."

The questions were hurling at me. What am I interested to do? What do I do each day to do what I love? If I didn't have to worry about my finances What could I do everyday? What are my strengths? How do I get to know more about? Every thing brought me to a single point that is the study of magic. I was destined for this. It's my magic gift, for the love of God.

The truth is, I didn't leave my job as a corporate employee the next day. The ideal time to search for the next job is once you're employed. When I was free, I set about organizing all my notes and books. I conducted research. I contacted the Universe. I spoke with other witches. I also made calls to other witches around the world via Skype calls. I also tried to translate all of my research into something encompassing but also simple enough for the modern-day reader. You may have some of the data is in your hand.

I performed a banishing as well as renewal ritual to overcome my fear and replace it with enthusiasm. This was the start of my journey as an author. The money became the outcome rather than the end goal. It appeared at the time I was in need of it. It often came in strange ways I would never had imagined. I would think of an account balance in my bank I'd like to have, then something would happen and cash flowed to my checking account. It was the ritual of "My taxes have been paid," and a lump sum of money appeared to pay my taxes.

The subject of money is one that can be a bit tense the things you eliminate are more important than the things you want. To identify the money obstacles you face it is essential to take note of your emotions when the topic of money comes up.

You get a pay check and you first think that it's not enough to pay your expenses. The negative thoughts are reaffirming your unconscious programming.

It is a blessing to those with no negative emotions about it. Working brings you money when you are enjoying it. It is a result of self-realization.

There's a different way to think about money, however. Look at it from the perspective of experience , not just currency. If you need money to purchase something specific, such as the purchase of a car, make an offer for a new vehicle. What are you looking for money for, aside from paying off your debts? Why would you like to have to have a million dollars? What could you purchase using this money? A house? Request a house, then.

Happy Life

Magic happens only when we have the right attitude and belief system. However, with all the negativity that is happening in our daily lives How do we manage to never feel unhappy? For starters, the word "happy" is not the right word. We should strive for peace. be striving for. Happiness is a result of external sources. It's a response to events outside. Peace is a result of the inner or coming from within Spirit. Spirit itself, and comes from Nothingness. Peace is always at hand.

The path to peace isn't easy; it requires writing your subconscious's program. The subconscious is fighting back each step because it would like things to remain "safe" in the way they are. The unknown can be scary.

Some time ago, I discovered an effective formula for me. It's called Do what want, not what do not need.

It may sound absurd and absurd, but it's actually quite sensible once you look at it. Of of course, we're not talking about extremes such as leaving your job today or murdering somebody. It's about acceptable social behaviour.

Begin slowly. Whatever you do, think, "Do I want this?" If your answer is no, then ask "What is my alternative?"

Have you been eating your cereal at breakfast because you're eager to eat it, or because you're used to it? It's easy and convenient? What else do you need instead? Are you really craving the salad, or are you eating it for the health benefits? Are you actually looking to speak to your family members or do you just talk to them just because you feel that you should?

The first step to peace, and consequently happiness begins by asking you: "Do I want this?" and "Why do I want to do this?" When your answer is "I'm doing this because I'm interested in it. There's no other reason," you're on the right path.

The next step is not to make a fuss about the opinion of anyone else about the way you conduct yourself. Only do what is the right choice for you.

There is no obligation to answer the phone call from your family members even if you do not want to. They can call you back whenever you want to talk to them. Who said that coffee is bad in the evening? I'm craving coffee, and I'm drinking it.

I'm not going to the game. Do not go without me.

Who says yellow and pink aren't compatible? You're a fool.

It can be difficult to complete this exercise because your brain can come up with many reasons and reasons to not follow what's "right." It is likely that there is guilt as well. There will be pressure from other people.

When I stopped taking emails and calls during business hours My boss was angry. However, he grew used to it.

It's not necessary to provide a reason why you do not desire what you don't. "No" as well as "I do not want to" suffices. If you defend yourself, you're operating in negative thoughts. Allow others to adapt to your style and believe the process will.

I used to repeat my mantra every day till the "want" state was automatic.

I am.

I am One.

I love living my life every single day.

I only do what I need to do.

All my requirements are attended to.

I am thankful for my wonderful life.

It is.

You are an incarnation of God, a evolved spiritual being. The mere existence of the world of ours is sufficient to have the right to be and to get everything you wish for.

Let's discuss belief. If you cast an act of magic and you don't believe that it will happen could end the spell. How can you get yourself in the right state of mind? Repetition this mantra after you have finished a spell, or any time you want to make a switch from negative feelings to positive ones:

Isn't that amazing? It's like something magical has happened to me!

Repeat the process and imagine the outcomes you would like to see. The more positive you are in your mood you are, the greater your energy field's frequency is. This alone can ward off negativity. Changes that happen inside can affect the world outside.

It's also a crucial element for a successful life: faith. Faith helps us to believe in the future regardless of the fact that our present circumstance appears to be bleak.

If a relationship breaks down be assured that it's because God safeguards us from the pain of the future. You're most likely not the best partner for you. Or perhaps you're not prepared for an intimate relationship.

If your delay in your flight, God protects you from danger. Perhaps there was bad weather or, if you arrive, there could be a crash. By arriving later you are able to are able to avoid weather disasters and car accidents, or perhaps an armed robbery or murder.

I am confident that I have all-time protection and accessibility to Higher Power. If things don't go way that was planned it means that it's because the Higher Power is removing obstacles or preventing the occurrence.

Here's a prayer I was taught to pray:

God Please don't allow my desires overpower Yours.

Chapter 7: Other Words

Higher Beings

The higher World depicted by Gods, Archangels, Angels as well as Higher Spirits. to put it in a mild way it does not have a problems with overpopulation. Imagine a pyramid made up of three parts, and God at the top, like the Christmas tree star. The top represents part of the Higher World, where the power is concentrated.

It's like having the richest of the world, which is just 1% of people. They have everything and the finest food (energy) and the most luxurious homes, and no crime. everything is gorgeous and comfortable.

The next section will be our Middle World, which is an intermediate in between our Higher World and Lower Worlds. The human race is born Souls and Spirits belonging in the Higher World. However, the way of life is of degrading Souls and contaminating the Spirit's energy

Spirit which means that the frequency is turned down. The majority of people don't know how to get back in their Higher World.

Lower Beings

It is believed that the Lower World is represented by demons Dark Gods, demons, spirits and lower beings of dead humans who could not be elevated onto higher levels of the Higher World - and Lucifer himself obviously. In the Lower World is overpopulated and filled with hunger and poverty at the very least of energy. The lower spirits only get the rotten leftovers that they take from humans.

Since lower beings don't possess an individual body, they are able to attach themselves to living human beings as parasites. They're hungry, they'd like to consume our energy, emotions and feelings.

The positive side is that lower creatures can't be attached to any human. One requirement must be fulfilled: a prospective host's energy frequency must correspond to the frequency of the parasite. Humans have a chance to not become food. It is possible to be indigestible through increasing our frequency.

Do you remember the pyramid? There are higher beings than human. That means that humans are constantly in danger. And the dark witches who call on lower beings only contributes to Middle World chaos. When lower beings make their way to their own Middle World, it's a feast. Retrieving them back in their home in the Lower World is very difficult and, often, impossible. They fight in any method they are able to. In the end humans who host them become lower beings, expanding that negative field of energy.

Realities

Albert Einstein once wrote: "People like those with a belief in science are aware there is no distinction in the past the present, the future, and the past is just a stubbornly pervasive illusion. The concept of time, also known as is a figment of our imagination."

When Einstein unifying time and space with his theory of general relativity, in 1915, Einstein provided us a brand new method to see our Universe. A fascinating theory called"the "block Universe" theory asserts that time doesn't "flow as a stream" instead all things are ever-present. It is true that the both the past and the future are all present. Quantum mechanics proves this. Witches have known this for a long time and this makes forecasting what's to come. Witches can also observe the past.

Time is not moving. We are the ones who travel through the ages. The day your birth is visible. The day that Neil Armstrong landed on the moon is only a few inches beyond the surface. My grandma's days are still there but they're out of my reach due to her passing to the grave two decades ago. But she's still here.

The future is abounding in endless ways. I refer to them as the stages or realities. Every day, through every thought and move, we alter our outlook on the future. We can't actually alter the future, but we decide on different stages or reality. With 6 billion people making decisions that have collectively led us to the present moment.

There's a possibility that I haven't moved to California. I didn't choose the reality, and therefore, we're not part of it. However, it exists as a possibility decision. A stage was made. I chose to not "activate" the stage.

With every thought and possibility, a stage can be made real or unreal. There are endless stage designs, both past and present, and many more are being created each day.

The house of my father is several mansions. If it wasn't for it could I have informed you that I'm going to the mansions to make an area for you? If I do go there and make a space for you, I'll return to accept you into My presence and hope that you might be there with me. John 14:2 - John 14:2

What is this reminding you of? Isn't that the exact concept of many real-world scenarios or stages? Jesus Christ told his disciples that through faith, we all will be transported by faith to one of those "prepared" locations.

Let's look at it in a different way. While traveling, our destination is just a thought first. However, as we drive and follow the road markings and signs, we soon get our first glimpses at the town. We then get closer and can see the structures. We soon are moving across the town. It wasn't just there, the place was there for a long time. From our point of view it didn't seem to exist until we got there. We brought it to life.

It's the same with reality. When we imagine some thing like "I would like to visit The Bahamas," we create an imagined reality where we're somewhere in the Bahamas. If it happens or not, it's a different matter However, a reality is already being created as it's an option. Through faith, this possibility can be realized.

Question What if the future continuously shifts, how can psychics forecast it?

The psychics cannot predict the future for a long time. They only can see the future in the near future that's nearly inevitable. Events that are larger are more well-established in comparison to smaller events. It's like we're going in a particular direction, however we aren't aware of the specifics yet similar to when journey to a city that isn't known. We know there's a town there however, we're not sure the buildings we'll visit or who we'll encounter until we reach the city. A psychic could sense that we're heading towards an event prior to the actual event is established.

Reality Shift

This is considered to be advanced magic. Only white witches with a lot of strength can perform this feat. I've not heard of dark witches that ever shift reality. It's an enormous volume of high-frequency energy, which is just beyond the realm of dark witches.

According to the internet, this latest style in "reality shift" is more than an "out of body experience" as opposed to a real change in the reality. People say that they are able to shift their awareness to other reality and return. This isn't an impossible thing, but it's not what they're discussing.

Have you noticed that at times things aren't the same as they were when you thought they were? Maybe things are different than you remembered? You visit your friend and you see the latest painting. "When did you get it?" you ask. "Oh many it was a long time in the past." "What? It was not here last week!" Then you try to explain the circumstance. Perhaps you didn't even notice it? Maybe it was not there.

The majority of people don't see any changesor try to justify these changes. There are some who think about what's happening because things aren't the same.

And then there are those who aren't surprised because they're the ones that made the changes. I can tell when the reality is shifting, because I sense it. I'm dizzy, it's like losing my balance. It's like the moment a train shakes, but at a slower pace. When I notice it happening, and realize that it isn't me who created the change and I try to figure out the reason. If I actually did cause it, there'll be several things altered that I did not intend.

Don't panic. It's not a common occurrence. Things that are important don't change. We do it mostly for ourselves, in order to improve our lives. We are We are those who have access the Higher Power, the white witches. You are part of the group.

Let's examine the reality shift that is. Let's say that there's a scenario that I do not like. It's possible for anything to occur. I'm not immune to all kinds of things and I'm not able for every single thing that could happen.

Now, I'm asking me: "What do I want to occur? Did I "prepare the place?" Did I previously thought that this situation might be different? If"yes," then it is possible that I have the ability to change the perception of reality.

For instance, when I'm making myself ready to go on a vacation I envision gorgeous weather in my destination. When I finally arrive and it's raining. However, I "prepared the place" according to John 14:2 stated in the past, through thinking about the possibility of sunny weather. It means there's a real world that I can transform the world around into. So I do it.

I worked a real-life shift at an immigration bureau, after which it was discovered that I filled in the forms incorrectly. Re-filling it could be the end of a long and painful process which is why I moved the paperwork to where it was completed correctly, since I was sure that I had completed everything correctly. This means that a stage was already set up; I had to get it into place. The rude officer in front of the glass told me, "Now you know why it's not going to be granted," I thought, "We'll look into the issue." Then I settled down on a chair in the waiting area and completed the shift. Two hours later, I saw another officer with my properly filled out paperwork in before her. She was approving of course.

Chapter 8: Internal Works

Subconscious

All the things you've seen or heard can be stored away in the black storage of your unconscious. The conscious mind can only remember a tiny fraction of it, however, all of your knowledge is stored the subconscious. When we are conscious about how we decide to act and think in a way, our thoughts pass through our subconscious first. Our previous experiences and our beliefs influence our emotions, thoughts and choices. Two different people can look at the same issue but view it differently due to their lenses are different.

There are also strict lines. Every hypnotist will inform that individuals have specific limits that can't be violated. It is not possible to force people to perform a task that is beyond their limits. If someone is in a position to commit suicide under hypnosis then that it was not their hard line. The person can also commit suicide without hypnosis, even though they would likely deny being capable of doing so. It isn't plausible. We don't have a good understanding of what goes on within the subconscious. We only know ourselves superficially.

Everyone has their own distinct lines and no one knows who they are. We're usually shocked when we see someone act "out out of the norm." Do we really have any idea what was going on in the mind of the person? What if they didn't?

Each of these filters, lines of hardness and mental blocks alter the energy flowing from the consciousness to Spirit. Soul also responds to emotions by using subconscious filters. The trigger for one person might be completely irrelevant to someone else.

We believe we have told Spirit the same thing however, Spirit gets very different information. Then we ask ourselves what went wrong and why it didn't. It did work. It worked flawlessly. Perhaps you don't own a million dollar in your bank account because in your mind, you're not prepared to accept it.

Mental Blocks

Everyone is aware of what mental or emotional blockages are. They're obstacles that prevent clear thoughts and feelings. You've been doing great and then and seemingly without reason, you're shutting down. You aren't sure why you're unable to conquer something that is simple that you're annoyed and maybe even angry. You aren't sure what caused the issue or why it happened.

There are many emotional and mental blocks as well as emotional blocks, ranging that range from the "really terrible" up to "really strange." Most of the time we aren't aware the mental block in our lives. These are fears that we have in our subconscious or "installed programs" from our childhood.

Did your parents discipline you? Do you remember being scared to make a mistake in fear of being punished? Perhaps you're now afraid to begin doing something, consciously believing that you'll do something wrong and get punished.

Did your parents tell you about how money doesn't come on trees? Perhaps , now that you make a wish to get money, your subconscious makes an extra footnote that you'll need work to get it. Instead of dropping a sum to the person you are, Universe will give you an opportunity to earn the money, or perhaps even a new job.

Have you been left unattended as a child? Are you apathetic? As an adult, you may are looking for relationships that have unhealthy relationships, as it's the way your mind is programed. It's not intentionally; you most likely aren't aware of why relationships aren't working out or don't please you. You may blame yourself or someone else. However, the root of your issues is always your own head.

The world is full of emotional and mental blocks. Every person has their own set of. Recognizing and removing them can be a challenging task however it is essential for the correct use of magic.

The battle to eliminate mental blockages will be the most bloody fight that you'll ever face. All of it will take place in your head. However, it's still worthwhile. There's no need to fight every single one of them. Just take them each one at a time. With every win, your life will be transformed in a miraculous way.

How do you determine the presence and location of an emotional blockage? The way to identify mental blocks is found in your thoughts. You don't need to continually monitor your thoughts. You only need to focus on your emotions. If you ever experience an uncomfortable or unpleasant feeling take a moment to stop your activity and ask yourself "What do I feel and what's the reason for it?"

Are you feeling jealous? You are jealous because someone is more beautiful or richer? The issue isn't with them. You're jealous because you believe you're not. The reason could be in your lack of confidence. Perhaps you don't like yourself. What can you do to create clean magic with such feelings?

What makes you anger? Because people mistreat you? Why is it that it's even a possibility that they would treat you poorly? Do you have any kind or aura people are able to take advantage of? Does your aura tell you,

"Mistreat me, I'm an innocent person who is a victim?" Casting a protection spell when you are feeling this way will be difficult.

I'm sure this isn't the best way to go. I'm still working on my own block at the end of the day. I'm not happy just like everyone else. I'm human. I'm trying to figure out my"shit.

Free Will

The notion freedom of will been a source of controversy with witches for long periods of time. Some believe on the fact that freedom of will a myth and others think that interfering with another's freedom of choice is considered a grave crime.

I'm part of the group that believes that Free Will exists. My understanding is that free will is a subliminal mental process that is woven into our experiences, beliefs such as likes and dislikes desires and wants. People make their choices based on their mental states. Any act of violence that is committed against someone's freedom can be punished with consequences.

We've already learned about hard lines. Even when a spell doesn't violate any of the hard lines, it will still stifle your will person who is affected. It's a harmful program that is inserted in a person's mind, and in time, destroys not just the mind but also social and physical states. The person who suffers from it subconsciously realizes that he is seeking something, but is always looking for plausible explanations. This leads to an internal dissonance that can lead in mental breakdowns illness and social discontent.

At first the victim is convinced that it's not a problem regardless of the fact that others observe changes in his behaviour. When hypnotists demonstrate their talents at the podium, they force people to perform a variety of fun activities. They don't realize that they're doing something weird. It's that when they "wake up" when they realize they've violated their own will. In the short-term this violation does not cause permanent damage. The subconscious snaps back to its original form. However, if there's a long-term breach, the mind of the subconscious starts sending signals to indicate warnings that something's wrong. That's the sort of thing that will lead people to the mental hospital.

Witches who cast a spell that infringes on the free will of a person is bound have to pay. The pathways of energy for those affected are blocked and a new one is created, connecting the person who is affected and the solicitor. The solicitor will discuss the results to the person who is affected.

Making Magic for Someone Other than yourself

There are two basic rules to be followed when working magic for another person. First, get their permission. Thirdly, you must follow your Golden Rule: do unto other people as you would want them treat you. If you don't like this spell to be done to you, do not perform it to other people.

There are a variety of nuances you must consider on a the basis of a case-by-case basis.

An exampleis that relatives of an alcoholic seek out a witch to end the addiction however, the person isn't ready to quit drinking. In this scenario, the witch must decline. If she continues, it is an obvious breach of his own will, and crosses the line of dark magic. In the second, his mind will deny the spell, and come back to the witch in an unrollback.

There are a lot of people who complain and continuously seek assistance. They are always in trouble. They call you to cry over their latest mishap and request your assistance. They might not be aware they're being a "victim" at the unconscious level. They enjoy being in this state because it attracts attention. They're like emotional vampires that steal the positive energy of people.

Let's suppose that an emotional vampire approaches you seeking help for an illness. You seek permission to conduct the cleansing ritual to eliminate this disease. While they granted permission to do so however, their subconscious is anchored to the condition as a part to their persona. If they don't lose the condition that is their identity, they will become less themselves. What can they do to earn people's time and attention without having the disease?

This is the point where the spell is discarded and is then redirected to the witch. It's not just that the spell bounce back off the witch, but it also gathers even more negative energy the bounce. What does this mean to you, the witch trying to assist? Nobody can answer that. However, something could happen to you. Are you willing to take a chance on the possibility of that?

Lucid Dreaming

I have a fantastic connection with sleeping. I am asleep within 30 minutes of hitting my pillow and at night I am as sleepy as kittens. I have never had nightmares. The best part? I don't need alarms. Before I go to sleep I make myself aware of what when I'll be up. It doesn't matter if have an appointment to make at dawn, I'll get up enough time to prepare breakfast for the kids even on the weekend.

What is the connection between lucid dreams and to have to do with magic? Nothing. However, it is everything to be in the mind of our unconscious. Dreams are memories that are chopped into tiny narratives. Yes, they do come to pass however, not because they're predictive. They are a reality because we shape our future with each decision and thought. Also dreams aren't able to predict the future but they do create it. Sometimes. But most of the time, they display our past cut and diced in our current problems.

Lucid dreamers are among the fortunate ones who can communicate with their subconscious. The ability to do this lets dreamers influence and transform any negative mental blocks or negative thoughts.

I've had vivid dreams since I remember. For a long period of time, I did not know that the majority of people do not. It's to me like being in two worlds. however, the dream world is much more vivid and vibrant, filled with vivid colours and experiences that aren't present on the earth. I can fly over trees or even across the galaxy. I can dive into the depths of one's ocean and be able to see it all crisp and crystal clear. The real world is dull and dangerous in comparison.

There are three major stages of lucid dreaming. The first is the most conscious in the early hours in the evening, as the brain is craving deep sleep. At this point, if the dream veers off into territory that I don't like I can either get up or enter a new dream.

The next step is exploring. When I am asleep, I realize that a plot is boring. That's all I have to say, I'm done. I take off to see what's out there. It's fascinating to discover what my subconscious can reveal. When I was trying to find the perfect house in my real life I began to look for houses that I had seen in my dream world. What I discovered was that the homes my subconscious had shown me were in poor condition and not suitable for living in.

The third level is the God-level. Every day, around dawn, I make the universe, planets and people, as an artist spinning stories from nothing.

There's a higher level that I refer to as "questioning the subconscious." When I'm confronted with a question regarding something I'm dealing with I immediately go to my subconscious. I or stop a dream character whoever it is and ask them questions or shout at the sky in my dream to reveal the answer in a visual.

One of my shabby-house visions, an old filthy woman was spotted in a kitchen that was fitted with refrigerators that were broken. I askedher "Why do these houses look older and shabby? I'd like to have a new, beautiful home." My friend laughed. "You don't merit this," she said.

In that moment, I realized that, since I'd never been in a luxurious area, I was subconsciously thinking that I didn't merit it. I was an imposter an unemployed person from a third world country that was looking to fit in with the upper class. I needed make myself believe I deserved good things. If I did not, Universe would have not granted me what I desired.

According to research, everyone can master lucid dreams. There are a variety of books and methods. While lucid dreaming isn't required to be a magician I would recommend everyone to give it a shot; it's good for the health of your mind.

In-Between

Science refers to it as Hypnagogia. There's a small gap between the sleep and wake states. When the body twitches or two, sound comes as clearly-colored images appear. There are people who feel as if they're falling. Most of the time, this is the time when people are asleep. The "in-between" state of mind is an entrance towards the Universe. The mind is conscious, and the body is still but all thoughts and emotions are still asleep. Dream state (subconscious) isn't fully incorporated yet.

The state of in-between is the gateway to the realm of magic, to another worlds and to the creation. Everything is possible. When you do something consciously in this state, Universe responds to it. According to my experience, this happens as if our minds and emotions are not in the way. There's an unambiguous connection between the brain and the Spirit.

The subconscious never rests, although it is able to give in to the imagination. In a state of hypnosis, we imagine scenes that feel real and when in an imaginative state we believe they're real. We are enticed by the appealing to our senses with imaginative ideas. Therefore, the subconscious accepts the reality and transmits it onto the Spirit.

Most of the time, people aren't in control over what they experience in this state, however with practice it is possible. There are many people who experience psychic experiences while in the state of hypnagogia.

Through years of study I was able to keep this state to the extent I require it. As I begin to fall in bed, I glance at the dark behind my eyes and see how splashes of vibrant lights create patterns, all the while contemplating a picture. The car I dream of is on my driveway. Images emerge in the darkness. I wander around the car, rub it, then open the doors. I feel the polished steel and the cloth on the chairs. I'm at the wheel. I then let myself fall to sleep.

I repeated the scene many times and then went to an auto dealer. There it was exactly the car I wanted and color, with tires, and all of the whistles that I'd thought of. Everything was waiting for me to pick up, and at the exact price I had planned for. Thank you, Universe.

The state of in-between is similar to an imagination that feels real. It's possible to hear, see the sound, smell, feel the air, and even talk - it's exactly like the real world. This is not the same as dreams that are lucid. When I dream, I am aware that I'm in the dream. You can fly around, breathe beneath the water, or even spin out into space. Things are always unstable, continuously changing. If I see something I read in my dream, I glance away, only to see words that have altered.

In the state of in-between, I am sure that it isn't an illusion because it feels as if it's real. It's stable.

Love and Duality

The Law of Duality states that every thing has an opposite: the night and day as well as darkness and light hot and cold. The two sides always balance. This is what's known as the Law of the Universe. There is no way to have more negative than positive. If there's something positive, there's negative. If someone is having a good time and someone else is crying, they will both soon be crying although it might not be the same person.

Now , you might be asking: "How can I be generally positive while having to go through an equal amount negativity?" Not so fast. It is not necessary to live at the extremes. In all situations, you must try to find a middle option.

The middle path is known as hacking Love. Unconditional Love is a wonderful quality that is without opposition. Happiness is a result of an external source. We're happy due to a particular circumstance that we experience in our lives. Similar is the case with sadness. However, love is a gift from within and doesn't rely on anything that we don't already have.

God can only be Love. Without Love, all sin is.

Why do we even talk about duality? What is its relationship to magic? The answer is simple it's how magic operates. If you'd like to shield your self from negativity you have two options One is to utilize external sources of happiness to increase your frequency, knowing it will eventually return. Another option is to go with the middle option, which is to stay clear of extremes and to live in Love every day.

I call it "moment" to convey a message. To discover the middle route you must slow down and be aware of the moment as it really is. To achieve this, you have to be in Oneness. Meditation is a way to be One with all that is around you, and with the Universe. When your perception changes and you see not only the small portion of life that is in the front of you, but also beyond what is visible, you'll feel peace and Divine Love.

Chapter 9: Preparing For Ritual

In order for magic to be efficient, the magician should participate in an act of ritual that brings clarity to his thoughts. The magician should also think about the kind of energy he wishes to attract as well as the best location for channeling the energy.

What is an act of praise?

It's basically a sequence or sequence of exercises that involve gestures, words or actions and objects. The exercises are carried out in the sacred space of the ceremony, and performed in accordance with the exact sequence.

They are more frequent than you imagine. The national anthem being sung prior to the start of a soccer game is considered a formality. It is a formal ceremony, and it's usually built on the ancient traditions. This is not a deviance from the conventional model as there are rules to be observed in accordance with the law. It is also apparent that a lot of them have significant symbolic meaning as well as performance.

There are numerous rituals to choose from, ranging between prayers, rituals, and religious ceremonies, to cleansing ceremonies and coronation rites, nuptial ceremonies of atonement and dedications funerals for presidents, as well as inaugurations and numerous other.

The components and elements of Rituals

Formalism: They typically adhere to strict rules which do not allow any kind of deviance or improvisation. Formalism is evident in manner in which the magician and other performers perform throughout the show. There is a certain manner of speaking and a particular sequence which creates an atmosphere of volume and order, and gives a feeling of excitement and confidence everyone who takes part.

Traditionalism: These are generally built on time-tested and ancient practices.

It is essential to remain faithful to the original intent of the ritual for as long as it is necessary to be understood and achieve the desired outcomes.

Imagine the Thanksgiving feast as a classic American tradition with its roots within the American Puritan settlement.

Certainty: Rituals don't permit modification. The ritual is created through a dance sequence or choreography. You must construct your body to mould your mind into an ideal state for performing magic.

Rules of Governance The guidelines you comply with are the ones that govern you.

Regarding formality, the rules establish specific guidelines and standards to ensure that conduct is in line with the general attitude of mind.

The guidelines outline the standards that are acceptable and what's not.

Sacrifice: Magic, at its nature, involves a sequence of rituals which appear as if they were supernatural in the sense they are. When dealing with gods, angels demons, angels or any other kind of entity, there is typically a need to perform sacrifices.

It doesn't mean you need to make blood sacrifices or other similar acts however it could be enough to make sure you've got the appropriate symbols that represent your choice to donate a portion of your energies and your time God.

or "sacrifice" or "sacrifice" - and you make "sacrifice" to those forces that have to be working to protect your rights and freedom.

Performance: They're typically as a type of theater performance. They are infused by the spirit of theater which is true because every object and element that is used in a performance is symbolic and signifies something unique. Each one has a meaning that needs to be comprehended by the performer.

The reason for rituals is to fulfill the purpose of

In your everyday and religious routines It is important to remember them. Everything from the way you begin your day, how you commute to work and the way you deal with holidays or get back at work is routine. They link the past to both the current and future. They let us see the interconnectedness that we live our lives.

Magical rituals will transport you from the everyday routine of your life to a mysterious magical, mystical world. Sequences are designed to release the energy you require, to release with pinpoint accuracy to help you reach your objectives.

We are creatures of routine. It is normal for us to feel an innate sense of security with our routines. We feel safe and believe that everything will be in accordance with the rules of conduct whatever the conditions surrounding us. Even in the chaos that is our everyday lives , we are told we belong to a larger group.

They're packed with information of the past as well as traditional beliefs that span from mythological beliefs up to today. Consider this as an enlightened book that provides you with guidelines for living a dreamy life. As magician, you've got one goal or vision that you want to manifest on the world. The elements, together with your choreography, words and words and the environment and the objects you use, can be used to boost the power of your body. Then, they transform it into goals you wish to reach and that is the true magic.

For the Magus They are focused on reaching your objective. When she is performing these rituals she blends both the timeless and temporal into present and the future. She is a fusion of both the spiritual and divine, not known to the masses before her.

They offer you the chance to use the most energy of any method and continuously push the energy to reach your objectives.

Make sure you are ready for the Ritual

For magicians one of the primary steps you need to undertake is to become aware of the world surrounding you. If you're not able to discern the various elements what are you planning to do to control the forces and energy that come from the natural world? It is essential to be sure that the location you are in at the moment is able to create magic.

The actions you take perform will influence the results you will get. It is therefore recommended to select locations that permit an energy flow. Consider doing these exercises outside, and imagine that the energy of nature is flowing freely throughout the space that you work in. It is best to complete these exercises outdoors as it assists you and your colleagues realize that we are all connected through an unifying thread.

It is possible that the place you pick isn't as a result of the available space. Don't let that limit your options. Utilize the space you're given. It is important to ensure that the location you pick will be able to accommodate you as well as all those who are attending the event.

It is important to keep the item in a location that you've designed and is dedicated to the work. It is crucial to avoid distractions, interruptions , or any other distractions that could hinder your concentration or performance. Be sure that there aren't any devices or phones in your immediate surroundings. To create a tranquil atmosphere, you can make use of trinkets, scents, or similar objects.

Every seasonal ritual typically includes the use of decorations and symbols to represent the season that is being observed. For instance the Ostara ceremony can be enhanced by fresh flowers. It is crucial to choose top quality music, the right incense and other elements that are in keeping with what the ceremony is about.

These factors will play a key role in altering your perception and putting you in a positive mood.

In order to prepare for personal tasks, it's crucial to be in a positive state of mind.

It's the same for others in the group. The reason for this is that the thoughts and feelings of group members be a part of the group and their energy will feed the entire group. Everyone should set aside all unnecessary concerns and worries in order to ensure that everyone is committed to the same goal and goal.

Ritual baths prior to the ceremony are beneficial since they cleanse negative energy that's build up and keep the intention from being affected. It is crucial to include salt in the bath water to assist in cleansing.

Salt represents the concept for cleansing. It is also possible to include essential oils from all the world's natural resources. If you're able, soak at the sea or in a lake. If not, don't worry. Make sure you soak as long as you can prior to you go in the tub.

If you intend to take part in the event as a group it is recommended to create circles. This means that every participant is accountable for the outcomes and each participant is equally crucial. Participants must be aware of the reason for the gathering you've arranged and be ready to give their energies physical and mental in order to ensure that the goal of the gathering is achieved. If any participants fail to keep their enthusiasm and keep it that way, it will benefit everyone else to let them go. The worst thing you could have to do is have a weak spot that can cause a disruption.

Additionally the instruments and equipment are to be cleaned prior use.

Check that each piece has sufficient power to complete the task it was assigned.

Make sure you have all the tools you require before you begin creating the bows.

The next step to complete the ceremony.

Every ritual is based on a distinct procedure that defines each step's place to be located in the order of events and with a compelling reason. Think of them as meticulously planned plays. The alteration of the sequence of the scenes are not advised or the point is removed.

The different ones have their unique history. They are sacred spaces where the subsequent rituals will occur. The moment you begin your ritual will dictate how the remainder of your event will go. The ceremony will take every participant to the place in their minds that they were created to be and will bring them to the point of intersection between the physical and spiritual, where we are all one. It brings us all together in mind and spirit, allowing participants to concentrate on the purpose that led to the creation of one heart, which is the heart that connects us everyone.

At the beginning, everyone is breathing simultaneously, joining hands and praying to gods and angels who require your presence. If you are doing it in silence, you need to meditate or pray, and make use of the circle.

If the level of harmony is achieved, the next stage depends on the goal. You can make patterns, sing, drum or even dance.

You can contemplate, think or even create a symbolic image. Whatever you choose to do you do, make sure it is aligned with your goals.

Keep in mind to remember that the greater you use the senses and the more involved you are, the better you can enhance the energy needed to create a memorable event. This can include the burning of incense or music or music. As the energy levels rise the drumming and chanting will get more frequent and more loud. This is a good thing.

The final chapter of the tale is as significant as the beginning. It is crucial to craft an effective conclusion that draws attention of all magicians to the activities they engage in everyday. If the show fails to deliver a satisfying end it will be similar to the conclusion of a disappointing experience that is the form of a TV show.

Viewers will be left with an impression that they are dissatisfied and the goal of the story might not be fulfilled.

It is essential for you to bring the ceremony to an end , and then affirm that your goal was fulfilled in that it has released all the gods and spirits who were summoned to help accomplish it. Furthermore, everyone participants must

It is also important to ground yourself. After that take a break and sing a prayer to God or conclude the meeting by singing. Everyone should be aware that the session is not over and the purpose was communicated to everyone, and isn't going to be returned with no reaction.

Chapter 10: Purifying Purification

Cleanliness and purity are crucial for any activity with a magical element. Purification rituals are just one of the main reasons they exist.

Purification

This is the process of cleansing yourself from anything that isn't clean particularly prior to engaging in any kind of supernatural act, like cooperating with spirits or gods. It is essential to ensure that you're clean in your mind and body.

This is not just a matter of your personal appearance, but also to the items you include during the ceremony and the surroundings that you are performing it in. The expression "cleanliness could be the next step on the road towards holy living" can be used to describe the importance of keeping an uncluttered mind. Be careful when it comes to your actions.

A lot of rituals stress hygiene, even before the advent regarding germ theory. Eastern religions were always insistent regarding purity, both mentally as well as physically. Being considered impure in the context of a ceremony was a insulting notion. Another benefit of purification ceremonies is that people know that they're not at risk of contracting something via the actions of someone else. Impurities range from organ fluids and waste, to morally wrong actions within the limits of their convictions.

Purification is basically similar to banishment however it's more complicated as you need to prepare not just your home as well as yourself for your rituals. As per Crowley magicians of previous times needed to undergo rigorous purification processes that included not having sexual relations along with fasting and following extremely strict diets, as well as making sure their bodies were well-maintained and clean, as well as doing a variety of complicated prayers.

Don't be concerned about participating in the entire process, since Crowley says there's no reason for you to purify your self. Set the intention, promise to remain pure, and then you're finished with the tale. This is how you can keep your body and mind free of any thing that could hinder you from living the life you believe in. Crowley is the author of Magick IV: The Book IV:

The objective is to maximize the opportunities to make use of every possible force to the purpose of attacking. However powerful the force (by any measure) when it is used to accomplish your goal, ensure that you are achieving the ultimate purpose is met. [...]We must constantly examine our actions and be sure they are connected to the one goal.

In the case of Crowley, it was sufficient to do symbolic actions such as drinking or bathing. The bath signifies that the man has eliminated everything that is not compatible with his single goal. The dress indicates that he is wearing everything positive and is aligned to his purpose.

Banishment

The cleansing ritual eliminates any spiritual influences inappropriate for the environment where the ritual takes place. It encompasses both spirits and negative energy, which are the stagnant ones.

There are many methods to eliminate someone, but only one can make it as easy as you wish to create it.

Before you begin to make circles (which involves creating circles with you and other people), it helps to boost your energy flow and protect your security. It is vital to complete this exercise to ensure that you are able to shield your space from the forces of magic. The term "banish" literally refers to the removal of negative energies or entities from your space. It is vital to practice banishment as frequently as you can to ensure the altar or workspace is clean and free of negative energy and impurities, so that you can focus on your spells and magick.

Crowley suggests the ban of everything general, however, he recommends keeping it simple.

Other rituals require that you eliminate any negativity, as per the name. Crowley recommends that you do the ritual of banishing every day in order to ensure you're a true Thelemite.

Self-cleansing

It's not possible to afford a messy filthy, dirty, and untidy individual that is in need of clean and order. Be sure to take care of your possessions and yourself to the best of your ability.

The costumes you put on for magic are best kept clean. It is also essential to ensure that you are physically clean before putting on your costume and begin your rituals. Wash your body with salted water. Rinse your magical clothing by submerging them into salt water. Cleanse all amulets, crystals and other items with salt water in the hope of creating positive energy for the objects.

If you think this is too much effort, think about it essential to ensure that every activity or plan you decide to carry out isn't an ineffective effort in the least. In the worst case, you may be attracting negative outcomes or others who aren't yours.

The Ritual of the Minor Banishing of the

Pentagram

It is the Lesser Banishing Ritual of the Pentagram Also referred to as the LBRP

It is a ritual which was utilized to initiate individuals belonging to the Order that is known as Golden Dawn, and has gained more and more recognition in the occult world of today. It is usually considered an essential element in any kind of magick-related activity and it is essential to ensure that when you join with the Golden Dawn order, the instructions for this first procedure (apart from other rituals of initiation) must be followed prior to becoming a member of to the Inner Order.

It is believed that the Minor Banishing Ritual of the Pentagram is very energetic.

It is a series of movements followed by the chanting of specific words, prayer evocation, and creating a magical setting for you to experience more magic, or simply practice your regular meditation.

The purpose of this practice is to eradicate anything impure that is not pure, including all chaotic beings and all things that don't reflect the five elements of the classic magic. You'll require your magic wand to draw pentacles into the air, and then draw the power of the gods' names.

In addition, you'll have to invoke god names. Additionally, you'll have to invoke the gods which have the power to control all components of the circle to guard the circle and ensure its security.

The Lesser Banishing Ritual of the Pentagram and the Kabbalistic Cross have certain basic elements considered to originate from Eliphas Levi who was an French occultist. The text's source originates from the Jewish prayer, which is typically performed before bed. It was deemed the Jewish custom according to Jewish Rabbi Samson Raphael Hirsch in his book The Hirsch Siddur (1969). The phrase is as follows

The Name is God by the name of God in the Name of God in the Name of God, God of Yisrael in the Name of God. God in the name of God, God, the God of Yisrael May Michael sit to the left of me Gabriel in my left Uriel before me Raphael lying on my back at the highest point of my head in the presence of God.

The preparation for this Lesser Banishing Ritual of the Pentagram

Pentagram

Certain orders suggest that there's certain magical equipment needed to carry out the LBRP. However, according the Hermetic Order of the Golden Dawn the equipment mentioned above is not required. It is vital to know that the Hermetic Order of the Golden Dawn (Ordo Hermeticus Aurorae Aureae) is an underground society committed to the study and application of all things occult paranormal and metaphysical. It was founded in the hands of William Wynn Westcott, William Robert Woodman and Samuel Liddell Mathers and they are all Freemasons.

It is something to be thinking about when you are looking to embark on the most relaxing pentagram banishing procedure:

The altar should be set in the middle of your room. This is in the area where your instruments that represent each element are situated.

Dress in a formal dress like an afghan gown, or another attire that is intended to perform rituals, i.e. the dress is used only by magicians.

The weapon of the ritual is a sword that is also called dagger (the athame is a good choice to accomplish this) as well as a wand, should you prefer. The function of this tool is drawing various gestures at locations on the kabbalistic cross. It is also required to draw the pentacles and also an arc that connects each point.

The Process

In accordance with guidelines of the Golden Dawn guidelines, the Pentagram Minor Banishing Ritual consists of three parts , and must be carried out in the order indicated below.

1. It is also known as The Qabalistic Cross: This can be repeated once it has been accomplished by LBRP. The idea of this is to make an astral cross that is based on the work created by Physical Magus. Every point on the cross is that of the Sephiroth in the Tree of Life. (The Sephiroth, which are emanations are the 10 qualities from the Qabalah through which the

Infinite manifests itself as it continues to make all physical and other realms of spirituality).

2. The formulation of the pentacles/pentagrams: You will draw a pentacle of banishing earth for the purpose of the Banishing Ritual, or you will invoke a pentacle when doing an Invocation Ritual by drawing the pentacle in the air at the four cardinal points, and calling the name of God that coincides with each point: YHVH for the East, ADNI for the South, AHIH for the West, and AGLA for the North. As part of this ritual, you eliminate and invoke four of the elements of Water Air, Fire and Fire, along with Earth according to exactly the same order. The final step is when it is the time to join your pentagrams to form a circle you draw on the air.

3. The Invocations of your Deities as well as Archangels In this moment, you'll invoke all of the Archangels in the proper sequence: Raphael, Gabriel, Michael and Auriel (or Uriel), and ask for their assistance when you see their pictures in your mind's eyes from every single point on your cards.

If you are of the opinion that Judeo-Christian names aren't the best choice, you could replace your personal names with the names from those of Archangels and God as well as God and the Kabbalistic Cross. For instance rather than using names like The Tree of Life, you might prefer to utilize names that are based on the Eastern Chakra system. Instead of using gods or names used by God and God or and the God of Heaven is able to repeat your own personal mantra instead. The majority of Thelemic magicians generally invoke the name of Aiwass from their heart when performing the Qabalistic crossover.

This is a sign of their devotion to the knowledgeable Liber AL vel Legis which often is referred to as The Book of the Law that is the main sacred text of The Law of Thelema. One of the most important things to remember is that magick is a personal issue.

Be sure to do what you'd like to achieve. Find the strengths that you have in you and follow this method.

Three kinds of invocation. There are three types of. Invocation is the act of calling on divine or gods, as well as forging an connection with the gods or divine being. According to Crowley The two factors listed below are essential to a successful invocation. The first involves "fire during your prayer" and the other is "invoking often." When you pray, perform chanting, dancing or singing or whatever you do to invoke the spirit, you raise your frequency to ensure that it is in sync with your own. This increases the chance of your prayers to be successful more. It's not enough to pray or chant; what Crowley is saying by inflaming your prayer is that you should let your heart burn. See the passion burn inside your soul and heart. Feel the divine flame on your body while you pray and apologies to God. God you'd want to connect with.

Then, you can use the expression "invoke frequently," for, like everything else repetition is the most effective method of improvement. If you practice and keep improving, you'll be more proficient at establishing the mindset that permits invoking. Each session is quicker as well as more relaxed than previous and you'll discover yourself after you've learned the method.

Crowleys consider that every kind of invocation can be more effective than other magic acts because it gives you an opportunity to invoke your inner self as well as your Holy Guardian Angel should you want to. After you called your Inner Self to the forefront it is simpler to determine what your true purpose is. Here's the definition provided by Crowley of the experience that is magical

"The brain expands to the point that it stops being fully aware. The magician must surrender to the power that, although it is within his own physical body as well as his mind it is not the state that his normal mental state refers to as "I." As the poet, love and artist let themselves be swept off by the impulse of creativity as well as wonder too does magick."

The invocation is essentially a call to the qualities that a person can offer. Invocations are generally a form of worship. It is important to offer your life to God to ensure that the god you choose can be present in your daily life to bless you.

"Three Methods of Invocation" by Crowley "Three Techniques for Invocation". Three Methods of Invocation

The book Magick (Book 4.), Crowley discusses the three primary kinds of invocation. Crowley declares that in essence, all three kinds of invocations are similar. However, each one requires the magician to connect with the Deity the magician is invoking.

Method #1: Devotion. The magician is aligned with God's divine nature. God by submitting to God by loving. The magician has to give up all that isn't necessary in order to live a lifestyle of worshipping God that he chooses, and can dispel any illusions regarding self.

Method 2 Method 2: Invocation. The magician becomes one with Gods through being aware of the aspect of himself he would like to invoke.

Method 3, Method 3 Drama. The magician's identity is joined with gods through their acts of love. It's difficult for normal people to surrender their own identity, just as actors have to give up their authentic self to be the person they play in the film. If magicians are able to do this, you'll find this technique one of the most efficient and efficient of all three.

God form assumed to be gods

The idea of gods being portrayed as gods is a distinct approach that magicians employ invoking their God. It is enough to utilize your imagination to imagine of yourself as a symbol to the god that you would like to be associated with. Imagine you are the entire concept of the god that you would like to associate with.

The best way to achieve this sense of connection to God is to position your body and parts in a way to reflect that god that you wish to invoke. As if the God's form blends with yours and is surrounded by your body in order to become the perfect representation of God.

After you're done when you're done, you can sing your name or "vibrate" you name front of God.

Keep it inside your body. The god's spirit is a part of your body, mind , and your soul. Be aware that you are god.

Get ready

There is no reason to emphasize the importance of ensuring that you're prepared prior to making any attempt the invocation of any god, or spiritual. It is crucial to ensure the heart of your cleansed and the space that you'll perform your ritual in is cleaned. It is essential never to summon a naughty spirit, or even to resist the spirit you would like to work with.

You should be ready for the future. Anything that isn't relevant to your goal should be eliminated. Do not let it distract you from the mission you're currently pursuing.

You should be at the centre of your being. To achieve this, make a smudge of the place you'd want to invoke within you. You can also sing while blurring your eyes for a greater frequency of your chant and get yourself into a state which is receptive to the prayers.

Consider your goals that you wish to accomplish through the invocation ceremony. What is the purpose that you're asking the god? What are the goals you want to accomplish by allowing the attributes from this god be your own personal traits? Make this a top priority on your thoughts, and do it with full confidence and trust that you'll achieve what it is. Begin by focusing your mind to gratitude and believing in the knowledge that your objectives are getting accomplished. Positive and positive outlook can help you get the results you want and you won't be dissatisfied or distracted.

"The Art of Divination

Definition of Divination

One of the most well-known adept's talents and skills is divination. The goal of divination is gathering data that aids their abilities as magicians in the the course in their Great Work, where they will eventually be able to surpass themselves.

Beyond the sound that is heard to your ears, there's an array of mental faculties that you can use in order to acquire the most precise and profound knowledge and insights by using symbols. Divination refers to the method of getting knowledge through infinite wisdom.

Divination vs. Divination

It's not the same thing as divination. If you engage in a discussion with a divination expert the person is trying to predict what you're likely to experience over the coming days. It differs from other divination techniques because it's more about understanding the character of the situation or the person. It provides an understanding of how people are drawn to places, people and things. Armed with this information you'll be more able to make better choices for yourself.

In every religion and in all cultures across the globe there are a variety of ways to use it. In the West the majority of occultists look to astrology to learn about the impact of the motions of the planets on us. Tarot is a deck that contains 78 cards each with their own significance. They also make use of the method of bibliomancy. This involves using an e-book, such as The Bible or Bhagavad Gita or I Ching or Liber Legis and then opening it up to seek out random spaces and geomancy, when the earth is carved with random patterns or paper to make 16 patterns. created.

Divination: Personal and subjective

In estimating the significance of a decision taken by diviners, one must be ready to be prepared for more than the myriad of mistakes inherent within the procedure. Its wisdom does not put them in a position to make more than what is offered. It is not enough for them to last. Of course, it's impossible to be certain that an important factor is not being ignored. [...] Theoretically, it is foolish to think that the Oracle is trustworthy."

The meaning you attach to the meaning of the symbol. If you're using your dreams to help divinate it is believed that fire is a symbol that represents danger to one person while for others, it could be a symbol of regeneration or a fresh beginning. The meaning behind dreams is identical no matter what method you employ to divinate which is Tarot, Runes or Scrying.

Practical divination exercises

Divination by scrying

The term "scrying" is commonly used to describe crystal gazing, oculomancy or hydromancy.

It's a long-standing method of discovering. If you've ever been to the scene in the film where the gypsy looked into a glass ball the scene of scrying is exactly identical, but it is not associated with the ability to predict the future. There is no way to predict the future. However, it is feasible to speculate using current information.

The meaning behind "scrying" is evident at "scrying," which is Old English descry, which means "to expose" or "to reveal the specifics." It's the act of showing what's hidden from our eyes or via our second eye. It's a symbol for the ability of our eyes to see things we don't necessarily observe using our five senses.

This practice first came into prominence in the latter part of the 10th century. It is documented in the Shahnameh which is one of the longest-running Persian writing. As Christianity began to grow divination in all forms was deemed "diabolical". This seems a bit odd as in all cultures there's always been a method of divination dating all the way back to Egyptians who relied on oil to get details regarding their environment. It was Native Americans who used smoke to uncover mysteries.

When you practice scrying you will be able to communicate to your subconscious mind and other dimensions that go beyond physical. It is possible to discover the nature of your identity and the things you're doing here. If you're looking to discover the truth about your True Will it will be extremely useful. It will help you identify your goals and objectives.

What is your chanting style?

1. Find a quiet spot where you are able to work uninterrupted. 2.

2. 2. Make a peaceful environment that you're able to swiftly into a trance.

If you think it's beneficial to have an area with a dim light and would prefer blinds that are closed, shut them. If you believe that exposure to sunlight is beneficial, then take the blinds off. It is suggested to begin meditation before beginning.

2. Make sure that you are certain of your objectives. It is more likely that you will receive the answers you'd prefer to receive. Make your goals clear within your head.

3. Study the subject you've selected, like Crystal ball, Fire Mirror, or even water. The trance can intensify. This is normal.

In a matter of minutes, it is possible to view pictures. Shadows,

Shapes, silhouettes, and silhouettes. You can see blurred images or flashes that shine. If you look at these pictures it is possible that you are present with dates, locations and times which are crucial to what you are seeking to accomplish. Do not try to search for something that isn't present. Let it flow effortlessly.

4. After the session has ended Take a moment to record what you've observed and then write down the specifics of your event.

It's normal to feel scared of what you notice at first. To conquer this fear, you need to ground yourself so that you be more attuned to your body. permitting the energy of the Earth to move through your feet as well as other areas of your body to help to strengthen your body. Relax and be aware that although you are able to see things, it doesn't mean that you're within the realm of your mind. Make a prayer to God to safeguard your life.

Dowsing using a dowsing pendulum

The pendulum must not be overlooked as it is an effective way of determining the truth about what's taking place. It's not just efficient and efficient however, it's easy to construct at home, using just some strings and an lock with eyes through which strings pass.

A dowsing pendulum may be made of a crystal or rock that can be hung on the other side of the string, or at the other end of a rope. It is able to provide insights at many levels, whether you're spiritual or searching for something that is underground. It could connect you to your Akashic archives, that provide answers to your most pressing questions.

If you ask a question the subconscious mind will be able respond by using the nerve endings of your fingers. They will move to respond , and your body will show its own self what it is aware of.

How do I utilize the pendulum

1. Select the best pendulum. You can certainly make one with strings and a key, however when you are looking for something that can get you to a certain mindset, it's recommended to take a close review of what you would like to create as the pendulum. What type of material would you like to build it with? If you're planning to create crystals, what kind? Look for the one that means what you most. You could go to an antique store, keep them all , and decide which one is the most resonant.

2. Clean your pendulum. It is important to rid it of any negative energy that has been trapped in it. You can clean it with salt water, lay it on the ground for a few days or use the small smudge stick. If you notice it's clear, you must begin making changes.

3. Find a way to connect to your pendulum. It's a simple process but it requires patience and determination like a real-life relationship. You're trying to figure out the messages that

your mind sends you and you wish to know the language spoken by your subconscious mind. In order to do this, you need to be asking questions. Begin by taking an inhalation to calm yourself and feel more grounded. Find direction and help by praying to the gods, your inner self or singing. Look for the most authentic answersand the most precise answers.

Ask questions to learn exactly what the meaning is when you are hearing "yes", "no" and "maybe".

You can respond "yes" through moving forward and backwards, but only in any direction. To comprehend the significance behind every direction, you could simply say "Show you are a yes" and then look around. You can then say.

"Show me the reasons" and then let him show. Then, ask to him "Show me the possibilities" and then watch. After that, thank him.

Another alternative is to ask questions that provide an objective solution, e.g., "Am I an Asian man or an Asian woman?" "Is the sky blue or green? blue?" Or "Am you an adult?". You should be aware of changes you experience every when you inquire "Am you an adult?". "Am am I an adult?". Make sure you complete this test or a test similar to the one described above, because it could alter your response in response to "yes" as well as "no" or.

4. Ask questions about your pendulum as you are using it. Make sure you sit in a comfortable posture. Be sure that your arm is stabilized and supported around your elbow. Keep your elbow in a relaxed and comfortable place between your thumb and index finger. Be sure to keep it in place to keep it from falling off your fingers. It is possible to ask the question you'd like an answer. You are able to ask whatever question you want... And then you must remain within the limits of reasonableness. You are able to decide if you have to attend an event, reevaluate your thoughts on something, or contemplate changes to your job. It will help you deal everyday problems and financial worries and also with relationships and spiritual issues.

Conclusion

When performing magic, it's crucial to remember this to do what you'd want to accomplish. Be aware that you're doing it to serve the primary motive behind each trick you create. If you perform magic, be aware that you are merely manifesting your inner desire to be in perfect alignment and alignment in perfect harmony with the Universe. It's the only important aspect you can accomplish, every single minute of the day.

It is crucial to perform your craft with a gentle and compassionate way towards all. If you're attracted by the desire to use your power to hurt others and even attracted to perform magic to make others feel weak, you must be aware that at the end of the day, you'll face the same type of treatment that you've received at times over 100 times.

The skilled magician has discovered that when practicing, she should be mindful of what is known as the Golden Rule: Do unto people as you would want them do to you. There is no reason not to recognize the wisdom you possess.

There are many fascinating aspects to be found in numerous books on magic, however there is one element which is most important throughout all of the books. This is wisdom gained through continuous practice, specifically when you practice meditation. It is vital that, regardless of what you do, you make meditation an part of your routine. There are certain lessons you won't find within the text. Instead, you'll feel these as you sit and contemplate, or as you participate in astral and yoga explorations.

If you're in your dreams and through your astral journeys you'll discover more about the true essence of our universe. Additionally, you'll discover new knowledge and techniques to enhance your spiritual path as well as the next. It is not possible to ignore the exercises you're doing. The more you do them, the more knowledge you'll gain and the more confidence you'll develop.

The tasks described in this guide are carried out using as little effort as is feasible. The reason is how they've been completed. When you work with magic stones, you must do it in accordance with your intuition. Your intuition will direct your to most efficient method for any ritual that involves purification.

Banish all blessings and become stupefaction at the power of divination and. The most appealing thing about this amazing life is that every single one is different. It is therefore essential to pick the one that interests you the most and ensures that your routine is something you be looking forward to each day.

The supernatural will start to show up within the realm of your daily life (and it will for as long as you continue to maintain your regular routine) Don't fall for the trap of thinking that you've "arrived" in the last phase of the bus that is spiritual. There's a lot to learn. There's always more to discover beyond the point at which you are.

www.ingramcontent.com/pod-product-compliance
Lightning Source LLC
Chambersburg PA
CBHW071125130526
44590CB00056B/1923